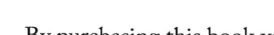

ISBN 978-0-260-43428-9
PIBN 10948061

Dedication

——

The Class of Nineteen Hundred and Ten

Dedicates this Book in

honor and love

To President L. Clark Seelye

1

Dedication

—

The Class of Nineteen Hundred and Ten

Dedicates this Book in

honor and love

To President L. Clark Seelye

To President Seelye

We cannot tell thee all we owe to thee,
We may not, in our blindness, know the sum;

We know that in our passing, day by day,
Thoughtless or troubled, we have seen thy face,
And felt a quietness pervade the place.

We know that in our faltering, thy voice,
Clear with enduring youth, rich with thy life,
Stern with thy purpose, calls us to the strife.

Thou hast held high the scholar's austere choice,
Yet thou hast made of it a gracious thing,
That it may fit our lives for minist'ring.

And when, with looking down, our sight grows dim,
Following thy rapt gaze we raise our eyes
To all the glory of the God-lit skies.

And now that, these years ended, we go forth,
A lamp held in that steady hand of thine
A-down the years to come we know shall shine.

We may not, in our blindness, know the sum,
We cannot tell thee all we owe to thee;
But for thy smile we give thee of our love,
For all thou hast taught us we bring gratitude,
To that which gives thee radiance, dedicate
Our spirits,—in that light we too shall walk,
And pray that our lamps catch a spark of it,
And that we keep them trimmed until the end.

Marion Keep Patton.

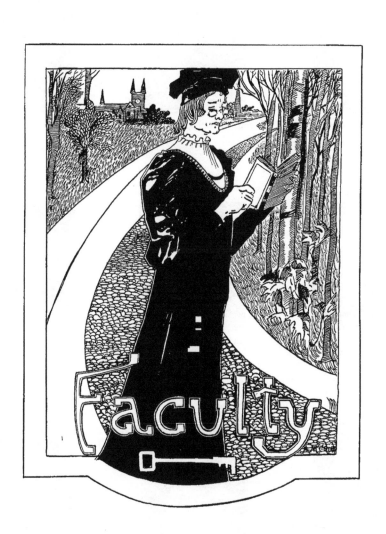

REV. HENRY M. TYLER, D.D.
Greek

JOHN TAPPAN STODDARD, PH.D.
Chemistry

MARIE F. KAPP, A.M.
German

ELEANOR P. CUSHING, A.M.
Mathematics

LUDELLA L. PECK, A.M.
Elocution

MARY AUGUSTA JORDAN, A.M.
English

HARRY NORMAN GARDINER, A.M.
Philosophy

BENJAMIN KENDALL EMERSON, PH.D.
Geology

DWIGHT W. TRYON, N.A.
Art

JOHN EVERETT BRADY, PH.D.
Latin

HARRIS HAWTHORNE WILDER, PH.D.
Zoölogy

REV. IRVING FRANCIS WOOD, D.B., PH.D.
Biblical Literature

WILLIAM FRANCIS GANONG, PH.D.
Botany

CHARLES DOWNER HAZEN, PH.D.
History

FRANK ALLAN WATERMAN, PH.D.
Physics

SENDA BERENSON
Physical Training

BERTHE VINCENS
French

ARTHUR HENRY PIERCE, PH.D.
Philosophy

(11)

ERNST HEINRICH MENSEL, PH.D.
German

CHARLES FRANKLIN EMERICK, PH.D.
Economics

HENRY DIKE SLEEPER, F.A.G.O.
Music

JULIA HARWOOD CAVERNO, A.M.
Greek

ELIZABETH DEERING HANSCOM, PH.D.
English Language and Literature

ANNA ALICE CUTLER, PH.D.
Philosophy

ALFRED VANCE CHURCHILL, A.M.
History and *Interpretation of Art*

JENNETTE LEE, A.B.
English

JOHN SPENCER BASSETT, PH.D.
History

MARY EASTMAN, A.B.
Registrar

HERBERT VAUGHAN ABBOTT, A.B.
English Literature

EVERETT KIMBALL, PH.D.
History

CAROLINE BROWN BOURLAND, PH.D.
French and Spanish

GEORGIA LAURA WHITE, PH.D.
Economics

CARL FREDERICK AUGUSTUS LANGE, PH.D.
German

ELIZABETH KEMPER ADAMS, PH.D.
Philosophy and Education

FLORENCE GILMAN, M.D.
Hygiene

HELEN ISABELLE WILLIAMS
French

(13)

Class of 1910

ELFRIEDE MARIE ACKERMANN
1918 Eddy St.
Chicago, Ill.

HELEN ALCOTT
124 Second Ave.
Upper Troy. N. Y.

MARY ALEXANDER
5304 Maple Ave.
St. Louis, Mo.

HELEN GERTRUDE ALLEN
17 Pelham Terrace
Arlington, Mass.

GRACE CAROLINE ALLING
Tyler City, Conn.

NORMA MacLEOD ANDERSON
New York

IDA BOURNE ANDRUS
Hudson Terrace
Yonkers, N. Y.

JANE BUCKINGHAM ARMSTRONG
102 West Liberty St.
Rome, N. Y.

LILLIAN FRANCES ASHWORTH
835 Hanover St.
Fall River, Mass.

(16)

LUCRETIA MAY ATWATER
195 Carew St.
Springfield, Mass.

ETHEL BENEDICT AYERS
Verona
Oneida Co., N. Y.

LOUISE MORSE BAILEY
39 East Broadway
Gardner, Mass.

ALICE WARDELL BAKER
236 Oglethorpe Ave.
Savannah, Ga.

WILMA C. BAKER
Seattle, Wash.

MILDRED SIDNEY BALDWIN
311 Perry Ave.
Peoria, Ill.

RUTH BALDWIN
56 Valentine St.
West Newton, Mass.

MADELINE ROBINSON BALL
41 Henshaw Ave.
Northampton, Mass.

BERNICE BARBER
619 South 9th St.
Minneapolis, Minn.

MARTHA BARKER
360 Monroe Ave.
Rochester, N. Y.

EVA BARNES
54 Elm St.
Westerly, R. I.

GERTRUDE MARTHA BARRY
55 Brighton St.
Rochester, N. Y.

FRANCESCA BARTLETT
Springville, N. Y.

VIRGINIA EVANS BARTLETT
1083 Delaware Ave.
Buffalo, N. Y.

HELEN CLEMENTINA BATES
295 Twelfth St.
Portland, Ore.

MILDRED ERNESTINE BAXTER
15 Rutger St.
Utica, N. Y.

MARCIA BEEBE
263 Foster St.
Melrose, Mass.

DOROTHY BELDEN
29 High St.
Northampton, Mass.

(18)

ADDIE IMOGENE BENNETT
Danforth, Me.

DOLLY CHAPLIN BENNETT
Bridgton, Me.

KATHERINE BENNETT
19 West 107th St.
New York, N. Y.

ELEANOR PERRY BENSON
46 Washington Square
Salem, Mass.

MARY DISBROW BERGEN
Haddonfield, N. J.

MILDRED ADIENE BERGEN
Freeport, Long Island, N. Y.

HELEN BIGELOW
69 Cedar St.
Worcester, Mass.

ANNA ELIZABETH BLODGETT
85 Walnut Hill Rd.
Orange, Mass.

BERTHA BODINE
Bellows Falls, Vt.

(19)

NELL STEVENS BOGART
Glenwood, Iowa.

MARION ELIZABETH BOOTH
Hotel Majestic
Philadelphia, Pa.

KATHRINE BOWMAN
Springfield, Iowa

OPAL MAY BRACKEN
403 West Pleasant St.
Corry, Pa.

ELISE LORD BRADFORD
52 Arlington Place
Buffalo, N. Y.

HELEN OSGOOD BRADLEY
21 Richard St.
Worcester, Mass.

LUCILE KATHARINE BRADLEY
Berlin, Conn.

MARY BUNCE BREWSTER
Warehouse Point, Conn.

GRACE CATHARINE BRIGGS
Industry, N. Y.

(20)

ELSIE NORA BRILEY
893 Pacific St.
Brooklyn, N. Y.

ALICE BROCKWAY
10 Sycamore St.
Worcester, Mass.

ELINOR GARRETSON BROWN
125 South Bridge St.
Somerville, N. J.

ELIZABETH BROWN
43 Hawthorne Place
Montclair, N. J.

KATHARINE CLARK BROWNING
Llewellyn Park
Orange, N. J.

MARJORIE LATHROP BROWNING
29 Lincoln Ave.
Norwich, Conn.

MARGUERITE ELLSWORTH BRUMAGHIM
34 North Pine Ave.
Auburn, N. Y.

HARRIET FREDERICA BUCKLEY
35 Prospect St.
Waterbury, Conn.

EDNA MARIA BUNNELL
396 Second Ave., South
St. Cloud, Minn.

(21)

CHARLOTTE BARKLEY BURGESS
84 Natchung Ave.
Montclair, N. J.

ANITA MERITHEW BURLEIGH
South Berwick, Me.

CAROLINE STINSON BURNE
Huntington, L. I., N. Y.

GRACE EMMA BURNHAM
1039 Mapleton Ave.
Boulder, Colo.

MAUDE EDNA BUSHNELL
Rockville Center, N. Y.

SUSAN FRENCHE CALKINS
1010 South 49th St.
Philadelphia, Pa.

HILDA MARY CAMP
98 Woodlawn Terrace
Waterbury, Conn.

EVELYN ISABEL CANNING
7 College Lane
Northampton, Mass.

EDITH NANCY CARSON
3 Pearl St.
Glens Falls, N. Y.

AGNES RUTH CARTER
4300 Park Blvd.
Minneapolis, Minn.

PHEBE CARTER
Carter Bldg.
Scranton, Pa.

MARY MARGARET CAVANAGH
Passaic Ave.
Passaic, N. J.

ELOISE RUGGLES CHANDLER
Manchester, N. H.

GERTRUDE BURBANK CHANDLER
Calhoun Place
Minneapolis, Minn.

GERTRUDE CHAPIN
41 South Fullerton Ave.
Montclair, N. J.

BRETA WILLIS CHILDS
9 Westland St.
Worcester, Mass.

AMY FAITH CLARK
3343 North 20th St.
Philadelphia, Pa.

MIRIAM ELLIOT CLAY
160 South Union St.
Grand Rapids, Mich.

KATHLEEN COCKLE
135 Randolph Ave.
Peoria, Ill.

BEULAH VIRGINIA COLE
Brewster, N. Y.

EDITH COLEMAN
1318 Lindin St.
Scranton, Pa.

FLORENCE HOYT COLEMAN
Newington, N. H.

CASSIE LOUISE CRANE
Groton, Conn.

ESTHER CRANE
Kenton, Ohio

INEZ HELENA CRAVEN
1414 East Howell St.
Seattle, Wash.

VIRGINIA CORYELL CRAVEN
Mattituck, N. Y.

MARGUERITE CRAY
1604 Stevens Ave.
Minneapolis, Minn.

(24)

HARRIET SNEADEN CROZIER
9 Upland Rd.
Brookline, Mass.

MARION AUGUSTA CROZIER
9 Upland Rd.
Brookline, Mass.

FLORENCE FREELAND CURTIS
310 East Harrison St.
Seattle, Wash.

LOUISE HADLEY CURTIS
48 Burnside Ave.
Crawford, N. J.

MARGARET ADAMS CUSHMAN
Munson, Mass.

EDITH LOUISE CUTTER
2040 East 79th St.
Cleveland, Ohio

MARGARET DAUCHY
870 Carroll St.
Brooklyn, N. Y.

ELIZABETH MATILDA DAVIDSON
South Berwick, Me.

LETTY LUCILE DAVIS
Hopedale, Mass.

ALICE FAIRBANKS DAY
179 Pleasant St.
Worcester, Mass.

ELIZABETH CORDELIA DECKER
269 Hempstead St.
New London. Conn.

HELEN BRAY DE LONG
Northampton, Mass.

HELEN CHARLOTTE DENMAN
Maplewood Terrace
Springfield, Mass.

FLORENCE JEANNETTE DEXTER
200 Trowbridge St.
St. Johns, Mich.

MARY DICKINSON
151 Rhodes Place
Newcastle, Pa.

MARGARET ALBERTINA DIETER
100 Mill St.
Northampton, Mass.

RACHEL ELEANOR DONNELL
West Brookfield, Mass.

KATHARINE VAN VALKENBURGH DREW
709 Douglass Ave.
Minneapolis, Minn.

ETHEL RAE DUGAN
65 North Vine St.
Hazleton, Pa.

MARION EDITH DWIGHT
31 Mt. Morris Park, West
New York, N. Y.

WINIFRED HENDERSON DYER
659 East 3d St.
St. Lake City, Utah

ELIZABETH EDDY
Auburn, N. Y.

IDA LESURE EVANS
17 Monroe St.
Northampton, Mass.

HELEN BARBOUR EVANS
17 Monroe St.
Northampton, Mass.

DOROTHY FAIRBANKS
St. Johnsbury, Vt.

MARGARET ALINE FELLOWS
44 Holyoke St.
Florence, Mass.

GUINEVERE FENNELL
908 Asylum St.
Hartford, Conn.

ABBE FRANCIS FERRIN
6 West 91st St.
New York, N. Y.

JUANITA EMILY FIELD
Berlin, Conn.

GRACE LILLIAN FILER
Killingly, Conn.

ANNA FINKBINE
2929 Grand Ave.
Des Moines, Iowa

SONAH MARIAN FRANK
1962 New Jersey St.
Los Angeles, Cal.

MARJORIE FRASER
2928 Washington Blvd.
Chicago, Ill.

JOSEPHINE ELIZABETH FRAWLEY
3727 North 22d Ave.
Denver, Colo.

MARIAN ELSA FREDERICKSON
22 East Gilman St.
Madison, Wis.

EDNA MAY FULLER
Springville, N. Y.

FLORENCE FULLER
736 Dayton St.
St. Paul, Minn.

ANNE GARNETT
319 North 3d Ave.
Phœnix, Ariz.

LOUISE KNAPP GATES
107 South St.
Auburn, N. Y.

MARY ELLEN GEESAMAN
1902 Paris Ave.
Minneapolis, Minn.

GRACE GERMAN
121 North 13th St.
Allentown, Pa.

EDNA THERESA GIBSON
9 Burt Place
Bellows Falls, Vt.

GENEVIEVE MARGUERITE GIBSON
176 E. Dwight St.
Holyoke, Mass.

HELEN STURTEVANT GIFFORD
2 Smith St.
New Bedford, Mass.

MARGARET LORING GILBERT
Dorset, Vt.

(29)

EDITH UPHAM GILL
Chattanooga, Tenn.

MARGARET CHURCH GILLIS
56 Franklin St.
Ogdensburg, N. Y.

CHRISTINE ALEXANDER GRAHAM
5145 Lindell Ave.
St. Louis, Mo.

LAURA MAY GRAHAM
405 Broadway
Pueblo, Colo.

FLORENCE ANTHINE GRANT
291 Prospect St.
Willimantic, Conn.

ELAINE PAYNE GRAY
16 Columbia St.
Cohoes, N. Y.

MARION CHARLOTTE GREENHOOD
330 Walnut Ave.
Roxbury, Mass.

ELIZABETH STONE GREGORY
1334 Forty-eighth St.
Brooklyn, N. Y.

ANNA MARIA GRIFFIN
South Hadley Falls, Mass.

JOSIE MAGDALEN GRIFFIN
South Hadley Falls, Mass.

EILEEN CECELIA HAFEY
88 Beacon Ave.
Holyoke, Mass.

BERNICE BARKER HAM
Lewiston, Me.

MAUDE LINES HAMILTON
63 Pleasant St.
Meriden, Conn.

MAUD BERNICE HAMMOND
Berwick, Me.

WINIFRED TRAVERS HANN
700 Springfield Ave.
Summit, N. J.

ELIZABETH BOYD HARDING
Whitehall, N. Y.

MARGARET HART
131 Maple Ave.
Webster Groves, Mo.

MARY LOUISA HARWOOD
Barre, Mass.

ALICE MABEL HASEY
Harwood Chambers
Minneapolis, Minn.

ELSIE HAYFORD HASTINGS
Swampscott, Mass.

FLORENCE CLARK HAUXHURST
205 North Walnut St.
Bay City, Mich.

MABEL FIELDER HAVENS
Toms River, N. J.

GERTRUDE MORGAN HAWLEY
1909 Seventh Ave.
Troy, N. Y.

MARJORIE HAYNES
1027 Mechanic St.
Emporia, Kan.

FANNY VOSE HAZEN,
Hanover, N. H.

GERTRUDE SEARING HEDDEN
20 North Walnut St.
East Orange, N. J.

HARRIET HELOISE HEDGES
Galveston, Texas

(32)

HELEN ELSA HEMPHILL
5 Courtlandt St.
Westerly, R. I.

CHARLOTTE AVERY HENDERSON
22 Meigs St.
Rochester, N. Y.

HARRIET BALDWIN HIBBERD
300 Main St.
Owego, N. Y.

NORMA ABIGAIL HORLIT
Carlinville, Ill.

IDA REBECCA HOLLIDAY
5137 Washington Boulevard
St. Louis, Mo.

FLORENCE ISABEL HOLMES
78 North Allen St.
Albany, N. Y.

FLORENCE ELIZABETH HOPWOOD
1912 Emerson Ave., South
Minneapolis, Minn.

ALICE GARDNER HOWE
Wakefield, Mass.

MARION HOWLAND
108 Eliot Ave.
West Newton, Mass.

ANNETTE LADD HOYT
Colby and Abbot Building
Milwaukee, Wis.

IRENE EMMA HOYT
18 Balding Ave.
Poughkeepsie, N. Y.

KATHERINE SCHUYLER HUBBS
223 Market St.
Amsterdam, N. Y.

MARGARET HUNTINGTON
141 East Broad St.
Columbus, Ohio

ELEANOR BUTLER HUTCHINSON
650 Center St.
Newton, Mass.

MILDRED INGERSOLL
911 North Church St.
Rockford, Ill.

DOROTHY GLADYS INGLEHART
327 Ten Eych St.
Watertown, N. Y.

LEAH IRELAND
Johnston, N. Y.

EDITH BERTHA JACKSON
Newark, N. Y.
4300 Park Blvd.

ELIZABETH HIGGIE JACKSON
De Pere, Wis.

ALICE BLANCHE JACOT
210 Ward Ave.
Tompkinsville, N. Y.

ELIZABETH WOODWORTH JAMESON
196 North Jefferson St.
Newcastle, Pa.

HELEN JEFFERS
6th and Chestnut Sts.
Leavenworth, Kan.

EVA JENISON
82 Lancaster St.
Albany, N. Y.

KATHERINE ELEANOR JENKINS
629 High St.
Keokuk, Iowa

MURIEL JOHNSTON
184 Sheldon St.
Grand Rapids, Mich.

FRANCES ADELAIDE JOHNSTONE
430 West 116th St.
New York, N. Y.

HELEN SWIFT JONES
434 Washington Ave.
Brooklyn, N. Y.

MILDRED KATHERINE JONES
4 Eagle St.
Utica, N. Y.

KATE KEITH
6421 Kentucky Ave.
Pittsburgh, Pa.

JOSEPHINE KEIZER
3227 Central St.
Kansas City, Mo.

GRACE GERTRUDE KELLY
Cheyenne, Wyoming.

EFFIE MARGUERITE KELSO
45 Suburban Ave.
Stamford, Conn.

ANNIS KENDALL
317 Nesmith St.
Lowell, Mass.

MARY ALLERTON KILBORNE
47 High St.
Orange, N. J.

CELIA ALLEN KIMBALL
93 Atlantic Ave.
Swampscott, Mass.

MARY FRANK KIMBALL
5309 Westminster St.
Pittsburgh, Pa.

HELEN CUSHMAN KING
47 Francis St.
Malden, Mass.

KATHARINE KING
624 South 9th St.
Minneapolis, Minn.

MARY CHASE KING
1425 Ertlaw Place
Baltimore, Md.

MARY MARGARET KNEELAND
183 Eighth Ave.
Brooklyn, N. Y.

EDITH COLLIN LAWRENCE
Grove Park
Asheville, N. C.

LILLIAN MARY LANDY
"The Puritan"
Boston, Mass.

LAURA FISHER LEGATE
210½ High St.
Newburyport, Mass.

ALICE BLANCHE LE GRO
Palmer, Mass.

RUTH LEIGHTON
177 Holland St.
Syracuse, N. Y.

3

LESLIE LELAND
10 Elm St.
Concord, Mass.

RUTH LEONARD
Wareham, Mass.

PEARL EVELYN LE VEQUE
113 West Ohio St.
Marquette, Mich.

JESSICA LEWIS
Cold Spring Harbor
Long Island, N. Y.

LEILA GORDON LEWIS
58 Saratoga St.
Cohoes, N. Y.

MARION BUCK LINCOLN
208 Canner St.
New Haven, Conn.

RUBY LITCHFIELD
9 South St.
Southbridge, Mass.

FRANCES SPECK LONEY
1621 John Ave.
Superior, Wis.

MARY ELIZABETH LUCE
Nashua, N. H.

MARGARET MARY LUCEY
18 Gothic St.
Northampton, Mass.

HELEN LUITWIELER
24 Dunckler St.
Newton Highlands, Mass.

MARY BEATRICE LYONS
4 Prichard St.
Fitchburg, Mass.

LAURA DITTO MacCOLL
Caledonia. N. Y.

MILDRED LOUISE MacDONALD
335 West Main St.
North Adams, Mass.

GRACE RUTH MacLAM
Ryegate, Vt.

FRANCES JOSEPHA EDDY MANN
34 St. Stephen St.
Boston, Mass.

EDITH MAGDALENE MANNING
26 Beacon Hill Ave.
Lynn, Mass.

LOUISE ESTELLE MARDEN
83 Boston St.
Somerville, Mass.

(39)

HELENE ALICIA MARSH
Boonton, N. J.

FLORENCE MARTIN
White River Junction, Vt.

MARY ETTA LOUISE MARTIN
547 Gorham St.
Lowell, Mass.

GERTRUDE VALÉRIE McCLINTOCK
1313 Fillmore St.
Topeka, Kan.

ALICE BROWN McGUIRE
3310 Washington Boulevard
Chicago, Ill.

GRACE BROWN McGUIRE
3310 Washington Boulevard
Chicago, Ill.

SALLY JANE McMULLIN
Watertown, N. Y.

ELINOR HAVEN MEANS
Middlebury, Vt.

MARGARET APPLETON MEANS
Middlebury, Vt.

GLADYS MENDUM
848 Beacon St.
Boston, Mass.

WINIFRED CHRISTINA METCALF
Clinton, N. Y.

GERTRUDE ETHEL MILHAM
219 West South St.
Kalamazoo, Mich.

HELENA FRANKLIN MILLER
624 Asylum Ave.
Hartford, Conn.

IRJA LOIS MILLER
424 East Penn. St.
Hoopeston, Ill.

MARGARET ELIZABETH MILLER
2941 Calumet Ave.
Chicago, Ill.

ANNAYMAR MILLIKIN
Eastport, Me.

EDITHA MINER
43 Crawford St.
Roxbury, Mass.

RUTH HOBBY MITCHELL
508 First Ave., South
St. Cloud, Minn.

(41)

EDNA CHIPMAN MOEHRING
205 Quincey St.
Brooklyn, N. Y.

CAROLINE LOUISE MONTGOMERY
Windsor Locks, Conn.

ELISE SHATTUCK MONTGOMERY
Frankfort, Ky.

GLADYS ELLSWORTH MOULTON
Greenland, N. H.

FLORENCE GRACE MURRAY
50 Church St.
Cortland, N. Y.

HELEN NEWELL
28 Portsmouth Terrace
Rochester, N. Y.

CARRIE WRIGHT NEWHALL
37 Cloverhill Place
Montclair, N. J.

ELIZABETH FRANCES NICHOLS
894 Clinton Ave.
Bridgeport, Conn.

TEI NINOMIYA
20 Hujoshimachi Kyobashiku
Tokio, Japan

MARGARET NORRIS
La Moille, Ill.

ETHEL LOUISE NORTON
Springwater, N. Y.

NELLIE WEYMOUTH NOWLAN
38 Deering Ave.
Portland, Me.

JEAN RHEA O'DONNEL
82 Linwood Ave.
Buffalo, N. Y.

ALICE STEPHANIE O'MEARA
585 Beacon St.
Boston, Mass.

ALICE MAY OTMAN
410 North Glen Oak Ave.
Peoria, Ill.

MILDRED VAN DER VELDE OWEN
335 Spring St.
Portland, Me.

CAROLINE DOREMUS PARK
Englewood, N. J.

MARGARET MARION PARK
4 Clinton Ave.
St. Johnsbury, Vt.

MABEL LAINHART PARMELEE
128 Mann St.
Owego, N. Y.

PHOEBE MAE PARRY
1039 North Lawrence Ave.
Wichita, Kan.

CLARA MARIE PATON
73 Idlewood Ave.
East Cleveland, Ohio

MARION KEEP PATTON
225 North Grove Ave.
Oak Park, Ill.

AZALIA ESSA PEET
Webster, N. Y.

VIRGINIA PEIRCE
"The Algonquin"
Dayton, Ohio

EMELIE MUNSON PERKINS
45 North Main St.
Rutland, Vt.

JANE HOLMES PERKINS
York Village, Me.

RUTH SHATTUCK PERKINS
York Village, Me.

(44)

MILDRED RUDD PERRY
Reedsburg, Wis.

MARY PETERSON
Manila, P. I.

LAURA KEZIAH PETTINGELL
16 Spring St.
Newburyport, Mass.

ONA EMILY PFLUKE
20 Summit Place
Utica, N. Y.

ANNE GARDNER PIGEON
139 Trenton St.
East Boston, Mass.

KATE STEVENS PIKE
Eastport, Me.

MAUDE ALICE PILLSBURY
Ripon, Wis.

ESTHER FRANCES PORTER
25 High St.
Northampton, Mass.

JESSIE WELLS POST
162 Ross St.
Brooklyn, N. Y.

(45)

FLORENCE MAY POWERS
17 Stoneland Road
Worcester, Mass.

NELLIE BERNADETTE POWERS
Lenox, Mass.

OLIVE FAWCETT PYE
240 Rutgers St.
Rochester, N. Y.

ALDANA RIPLEY QUIABY
27 West 86th St.
New York, N. Y.

ANN ELIZABETH RAWLS
309 Lafayette Ave.
Brooklyn, N. Y.

HELEN NEWTON REES
324 West 9th St.
Erie, Pa.

MARY LOUISE REILLY
65 Alton St.
Brockton, Mass.

JESSIE LEE RIALL
Walnut Ave., Rognell Heights
Baltimore, Md.

MARION STEVENS RICHARDS
Falmouth, Me.

(46)

WILMA RIDGWAY
669 Graceland Ave.
Chicago, Ill.

EDITH CAROLINE RIKER
111 Cleveland St.
Orange, N. J.

MARY FRANCES RILEY
17 Highland Ave.
Holyoke, Mass.

BESSIE KNIGHT ROBERTS
106 South 10th Ave.
Mt. Vernon, N. Y.

EDNA ALICE ROBERTS
Stites, Idaho

MARJORIE ESTABROOK ROBERTS
1704 Knox Ave., South
Minneapolis, Minn.

GERTRUDE LUDLAM ROBINSON
Carthage, N. Y.

FRANCES ROE
Augusta
Sussex County, N. J.

ANNABEL ABBOT ROOT
3911 Dibble Ave., N. E.
Cleveland, Ohio

(47)

MARTHA ERMINIE ROST
222 Twenty-eighth St.
Milwaukee. Wis.

ALMA SOPHIA ROTHHOLTZ
2108 Bolton St.
Baltimore, Md.

GLADYS ELIZABETH RUSSELL
Somersworth, N. H.

EVELYN LOUISE RYDER
Westdale. Mass.

MILDRED SAWYER
Rye Beach, N. H.

ETHEL MAY SCAIEFE
Eugene. Ore.

SARAH JOHNSON SCHENCK
Princeton, N. J.

ALMA CAROL SCHLESINGER
222 Ogden Ave.
Milwaukee, Wis.

ANNA LOUISE SCHMITZ
Waterbury, Conn.

MARGUERITE SCOTT
65 Ingersoll Grove
Springfield, Mass.

MARY BLANCHARD SCOTT
56 Bayard Lane
Princeton, N. J.

MURIEL SEELEY
Kennard Rd.
Brookline, Mass.

OLIVE LOUISE SEYMORE
Elmwood, Conn.

ANNABEL HITCHCOCK SHARP
Vermilion, Ohio

CAROLINE LOUISE SHAW
Ovid, Mich.

HELEN LOUISE SHERMAN
Fremont, Ohio

ANNA EMILY SIGAFUS
Stroudsburg, Pa.

MARJORIE ELLIOTT SIMMONS
912 Jefferson St.
Wilmington, Del.

JANET SIMON
North Adams, Mass.

FRANCES PIERPONT SIVITER
122 Dithridge St.
Pittsburgh, Pa.

BERTHA LOUISE SKINNER
South Swansea, Mass.

ELIZABETH SKINNER
Dunedin, Fla.

ELLEN HENRIETTA SKINNER
644 Lucas Ave.
Los Angeles, Cal.

ANNA ADELAIDE SMART
1407 Spruce Place
Minneapolis, Minn.

ELIZABETH ALLEN SMART
Cambridge, N. Y.

ANNE DAWSON SMITH
75 Brunswick St.
Rochester, N. Y.

ESTHER ANN SMITH
5135 Kensington Ave.
St. Louis, Mo.

ESTHER MARGARET SMITH
Wilkinsburg, Pa.

GERTRUDE COCHRANE SMITH
Inwood Place
Buffalo, N. Y.

HORTENSE EUGENIE SMITH
827 Washington St.
Hoboken, N. J.

MARJORIE DEARBORN SMITH
Ivaniston Ave.
Bridgeport, Conn.

MAUDE KETCHUM SMITH
Woodstock, New Brunswick, Canada

WINIFRED BARBARA SMITH
806 West Ferry St.
Buffalo, N. Y.

MABEL ARDRA SOULE
Hingham, Mass.

HENRIETTA SPERRY
32 Bedford Terrace
Northampton, Mass.

MARY ANNE STAPLES
Stroudsburg, Pa.

(51)

MARY HENRY STEEN
218 South 44th St.
Philadelphia, Pa.

KATHERINE STEVENS
Deep River, Conn.

ETHEL STIMSON
280 Harvard St.
Cambridge, Mass.

YEOLI STIMSON
Elkadere, Iowa

ANNA ADELE STREIBICH
620 Second Ave.
Peoria, Ill.

JESSIE LAUREL SULLIVAN
Brooklawn Place
Bridgeport, Conn.

VIOLA MARVEL SULLIVAN
64 Fletcher St.
Winchester, Mass.

ELSIE IRWIN SWEENEY
Columbus, Ind.

PORTIA MANSFIELD SWETT
33 Maple St.
Ashland, Ohio

MARJORIE TALBOT
31 Hutchings St.
Roxbury, Mass.

SUE ELEANOR TAYLOR
85 Caledonia Ave.
Rochester, N. Y.

EVA CEDELIA TEBBETTS
Berwick, Me.

CLARA JEANNETTE THIESE
Fort Wayne, Ind.

MARION THOMAS
Speelman Terrace
Rutland, Vt.

CAROLINE THOMPSON
124 Union Ave.
Saratoga Springs, N. Y.

EDITH THORNTON
103 Clay St.
Pawtucket, R. I.

RUTH ELIZABETH TUTTLE
43 Beaumont St.
Ashmont, Mass.

VERA BERYL URQUHART
3928 Russel Ave.
St. Louis, Mo.

4

JULIET ESTELLE VALENTINE
Coldspring Harbor, N. Y.

MARJORIE VALENTINE
4342 Ellis Ave.
Chicago, Ill.

MAREL VAN DEUSEN
South Catalina Ave.
Pasadena, Cal.

GLADYS REMSEN VAN DEVENTER
234 West 101st St.
New York, N. Y.

CLARA EVA VAN ESDEN
367 West 83d St.
New York, N. Y.

LOUISA GODDARD VAN WAGENEN
133 South 4th St.
Fulton, N. Y.

ANNAR MARIE WAIT
Jessup Ave. and 172d St.
New York, N. Y.

JENNIE GERTRUDE WAITE
105 Elm St.
Worcester, Mass.

AMY BARBARA WALLBURG
54 Dale St.
Boston, Mass.

HELEN MARY WALTERS
Wyoming, Ill.

FLORENCE WARD
1024 Madison Ave.
Albany, N. Y.

ANNA LORAINE WASHBURN
377 Marlborough St.
Boston, Mass.

MARTHA WILCOX WASHBURN
1112 Sixth St.
Minneapolis, Minn.

DOROTHY WATERMAN
162 State St.
Albany, N. Y.

CONSTANCE WATSON
511 Eighth St., South
Fargo. N. D.

OLIVE BEATRICE WATSON
912 Clary St.
Beloit, Wis.

MARION CECILE WEBSTER
Chester, N. H.

KATHERINE STURTEVANT WELLS
69 Garland St.
Chelsea, Mass.

MARJORIE WELLS
3753 Ellis Ave.
Chicago, Ill.

MAUDE EARLE WESBY
9 Horne St.
Worcester, Mass.

MARY JACKSON WEST
Wilmington, Ohio

KATHARINE LELAND WHITIN
Whitinsville, Mass.

ELAINE SHEFFIELD WHITMAN
109 Walnut Ave.
Boston, Mass.

EDNAH AUGUSTA WHITNEY
10 Sanborn Ave.
Somerville, Mass.

HELEN KING WHITON
71 Williams St.
New London, Conn.

ELIZABETH PLATT WILDS
Middlebury, Vt.

EDITH HOLMES WILLETTS
210 Prospect St.
Waterbury, Conn.

MILDRED CLAIRE WILLIAMS
Albion, N. Y.

MARION ELSIE WILMOT
134 Summit Ave.
Redlands, Cal.

ETHEL SOMERS WILSON
834 Myrtle Ave.
Bridgeport, Conn.

GERTRUDE ELIZABETH WILSON
1302 Pacific St.
Brooklyn, N. Y.

MARY GRUMMAN WINANS
Princeton, N. J.

MAUDE GENEVIEVE WOOLSON
Wellington, Mass.

CARRIE DELLA WRIGHT
Colchester, Vt.

ELIZABETH CURTIS WRIGHT
308 Myrtle Ave.
Bridgeport, Conn.

RUA LOUISE YEAW
3 School St.
Brattleboro, Vt.

(57)

HILLYER GALLERY.

Adams, Eva Bryant
Adams, Margaret Van Deusen
Aldrich, Helen Bursley
Atwater, Margaret Willard
Averill, Dorothy
Bailey, Alice Neal
Bailey, Sara May
Becker, Helen
Benedict, Dorothy
Benson, Myra Cornelia
Bickford, Mae Elizabeth
Birmingham, Beatrice
Blunt, Eugenia
Bowes, Jessie Reeves
Boynton, Lilian Farrand
Brooks, Ellen Rosette
Browne, Maude Leonore
Burke, Ada Ethel
Butterfield, Frances Amanda
Carlson, Hilma Cecelia
Carroll, Margaret Ethel
Chapin, Elizabeth
Clark, Julia Adeline
Clerihew, Catharine Forman

Cobb, Myra Elizabeth
Coyle, Virginia DuCasse
Crowell, Della Susan
Cunningham, Lois
de le Barre, Louise
Duffee, Doris
Falconer, Helen
Fay, Edith Marion
Fay, Grace Louisa
Fiske, Fanny Howe
Flagg, Lenora Enid
Forbes, Elizabeth Cornelia
Ford, Florence Stella
Ford, Helene Lillian
Gilbert, Kate
Gile, Miriam Richards
Goodhue, Frances
Grable, Katharine Lee
Gragg, Julia Alice
Gray, Mary
Gray, Ruth
Harber, Louise
Harrison, Frances Drake
Herrick, Margaret

Homer, Dora
Hultman, Julia Eugenia
Jackson, Mary Louise
Jones, Eleanor Genevra
Jones, Ethel Hannah
Kennedy, Caroline Cook
Kramer, Helen
Lane, Lottie Rachelle
Lehman, Lois Partridge
Luscher, Julia Gordon
Lyman, Alice
Malley, Margaret Cecelia
Maloy, Agnes Catherine
Mann, Edith Belle
Mason, Grace Elizabeth
McClench, Cora Christine
McKelvey, Gertrude Brownlee
McMechan, Erin Theresa
Mellor, Ethel Louise
Milk, Margaret Loduska
Milk, Mary Sherwood
Miller, Mary
Mindeleff, Natalia Victoroona
Mitchell, Anna Ames
Moore, Margaret Elizabeth
Morse, Katharine Duncan
Nichols, Minnie Louise
Nicholson, Carrie
Nye, Elizabeth Ellen
Osborn, Mary Louise
Ostram, Helen Margaret
Ozier, Margaret Lucille
Packard, Esther
Parker, Louise Lang
Parsons, Annie Keene
Pease, Kathryn
Phillip, Charlotte Alling
Phillips, Lura Madeline
Plaut, Florence Theresa
Richardson, Augusta Hortense

Roberts, Harriet Gertrude
Rose, Grace Beatson
Russell, Pauline
Schaffner, Halle Josephine
Schickle, Mary Dorothea
Schnierle, Sarah Elizabeth
Schwarz, Gertrude Florence
Seager, Olive
Searle, Annie Pier
Shepherd, Ruth Elizabeth
Sherwood, Sarah Emily
Skinner, Ellen Henrietta
Smith, Edith Frances
Smith, Emily Pauline
Smith, Helen Herndon
Smith, Helen Pitner
Smith, June Keith
Spencer, Bertha Elizabeth
Spofford, Grace Harriet
Stearns, Marion Landers
Stone, June Elizabeth
Sturges, Caroline Margaret
Sweet, Sadie Lillian
Tait, Georgia Belle
Talmage, Hilda
Tibbetts, Jane Nason
Todd, Marjory Caroline
Underwood, Marguerite
Vary, Grace Elizabeth
Ward, Julia Jennings
Ware, Louise Stevens
Weed, Hettie Barbara
Wesby, Maude Earle
White, Genevieve
Wicks, Grace Elizabeth
Wilbar, Katherine Latham
Williams, Florence Minnie
Williams, Octavia Emily
Willson, Inez Ora
Wintter, Cora Nanette

In Memoriam

✠

Jeannette Eliza Phelps
Carolina Underwood

FRESHMAN YEAR

On the twentieth of September, nineteen hundred and six, the great and glorious Class of 1910 arrived in Northampton. Of course we didn't really know ourselves as 1910, but that was our official title and it sounded well. So we trusted those who knew the ways of college and believed them when they told us we were a class and a very remarkable one as far as size went. We later found that we were remarkable in many other ways as well, but at that early date we were content with being regarded as a "phenomenal class" on account of our numbers. Indeed we secretly thought that this had its disadvantages, for we felt horribly confused and bewildered when we gazed about Freshman gallery and saw girls to right of us, girls to left of us. However, with the courage of the valiant six hundred we struggled through those first trying days of college, when we heard of more things that we were expected to do each day than we had dreamed of doing in the entire four years. We survived the perils and joys of the frolic and emerged from chaos at five forty-five, October third, triumphant and vociferous, a class with four officers of our very own.

To be sure it took us some time to get those officers, for at an early age 1910 developed a determination and tenacity of purpose that have since won her many triumphs in various phases of college life, but which have more than once impeded the progress of parliamentary rule in class meetings. But the record-breaking length of our first meeting merely strengthened our own and everybody else's opinion of our unusual qualities and when the campus house dinner bells were sounding a cheery summons, we separated, well content with ourselves and with our President.

Then Sophomore Reception! There never was one equal to it. 1909 played hostess most charmingly and we were hauled and jammed from one part of the Students' Building to another, in the fond delusion that we were dancing. But 1909 did their best for us and we consoled ourselves for our tattered ribbons and torn frocks by the thought that the jam was due entirely to the vast size of our remarkable class. Anyway we had a wonderful time and when "Home, Sweet Home" sounded, we scattered with happy hearts, feeling that we really must be a factor to be reckoned with in college since the Sophomores had been so impressed with us as to give a reception for our President.

We were glad that the Reception was followed by Mountain Day and that no nine o'clock math. classes summoned us forth at an abominably early hour. And Mountain Day, like everything else in that eventful year, was a record-breaker. Dame Nature seemed bent on testing our sporting spirit, and sent rain, snow, sleet and hail to dampen our ardor. Regardless of such trifles, we scattered throughout the land in trolleys, express wagons, or by way of "Shank's Mare," and if the storm blotted out the beauties of the landscape, the coffee and bacon, when we finally persuaded our fires to burn and the water to boil, were doubly delectable. Then, too, such weather was no more than we expected. We had heard dire tales of New England winters before penetrating the wilds of Hamp—many of us cherished fond hopes of seeing fur coats drifting our way at Christmas as a result of these details of life in the frozen north.

We were justified in our expectations of a long winter, for by the time we separated for Thanksgiving we had tested the joys of sleighing, and soon after the last remnants of the turkey that had cheered the sojourners in Northampton had made its last appearance in the sorry guise of Campus House hash, the clanking of skates might have been heard Paradiseward. 1908 skated as well as she did everything else and of course 1910 desired to emulate her in that—as in everything else—so that skating was wildly popular all winter, the enthusiasm culminating in the grand ice carnival. That was an event to be long remembered. Everyone went. It was a great success and supplied a topic for numberless home letters. The proceeds—memory fails, but doubtless they were used to swell the library fund.

For though our days and evenings were spent batting and fussing to such an extent that the Faculty looked anxious and the Seniors felt called on to remonstrate on Rally Day with the poignant suggestion,

> "Though we're not much on knocking,
> The way you fuss is shocking,"

still there was a vein of deep seriousness underlying all the joys and excitements of these Freshman days—the Library. It seemed a purpose, even at that early date, and steadied our minds and morals as we carefully hoarded our pennies and dimes that we might add to the fund—and incidentally get in at all the dances, plays and basket-ball games to which admission was charged. And now that Library—"but that is another story."

And Rally Day! It seems as though Rally Day banners must have waved over the legs of the Thanksgiving turkey, but it is safe to say that in accordance with the established order of things, Christmas and mid-years intervened, and statistics show that a few people "over-worked" in that period and were not present to swell the chorus on Rally Day, but there were enough of us to astonish our elders with our challenging "Smash Bang!" under the leadership of our Esther Ann. In the afternoon, when the score stood 31-16, the best Sophomore-Freshman score made in years, our enthusiasm was almost more than we could survive and we sang "Ach du Liebe" to "our Dorothy Waterman" and "the whole team" with all our might. We certainly were happy and when Big Game Day came, our team again showed 1909 and the Junior coaches that 1910 could play basket-ball.

And then before we had time to think of such a thing as the serious work to which we were told the winter term was always devoted, spring term was upon us. It rained and then it rained again, and then it rained some more. We had heard wonderful tales of spring term and we felt that we had traditions to live up to, so we each decided that

"It is not raining rain to me,
It is raining violets,"

and proceeding on that principle batted as wildly and as hilariously as though the sun had beamed upon us every day.

All too quickly the spring passed. We watched the Seniors give the steps to the Juniors and wondered if it really could be "better to give than to receive." We went on final bats, tucked in exams here and there, criticized "Much Ado" and then being cordially urged to leave town, we hustled our raiment into our trunks and departed with a host of happy memories and the joyous prospect of seeing our "sister 1908" again in September.

MARY ALLERTON KILBORNE

A BACON BAT

Class Officers

Senior Officers

President	.	.	.	.	CAROLINE DOREMUS PARK
Vice-President	.	.	.	.	HELEN CHARLOTTE DENMAN
Secretary	.	.	.	.	JESSIE WELLS POST
Treasurer	.	.	.	.	ELIZABETH MATILDA DAVIDSON
Historian	.	.	.	.	MARION KEEP PATTON

Freshman Officers

President	.	.	.	.	KATHRINE BOWMAN
Vice-President	.	.	.	.	HELEN BIGELOW
Secretary	.	.	.	.	MARION LANDERS STEARNS
Treasurer	.	.	.	.	ESTHER PACKARD
Historian	.	.	.	.	MARY ALLERTON KILBORNE

Sophomore Officers

President	.	.	.	.	MARY ALLERTON KILBORNE
Vice-President	.	.	.	.	CAROLINE DOREMUS PARK
Secretary	.	.	.	.	MARY ALEXANDER
Treasurer	.	.	.	.	LOUISE KNAPP GATES
Historian	.	.	.	.	VIRGINIA CORYELL CRAVEN

Junior Officers

President	.	.	.	.	HELEN BIGELOW
Vice-President	.	.	.	.	KATHERINE BENNETT
Secretary	.	.	.	.	JANE HOLMES PERKINS
Treasurer	.	.	.	.	HENRIETTA SPERRY
Historian	.	.	.	.	MARY FRANK KIMBALL

The Library

SOCIETIES

Dreka.

Phi Beta Kappa

HELEN GERTRUDE ALLEN
LOUISE MORSE BAILEY
ALICE WARDELL BAKER
BERNICE BARBER
AGNES RUTH CARTER
EDITH COLEMAN
FLORENCE FREELAND CURTIS
MARGARET ADAMS CUSHMAN
HELEN CHARLOTTE DENMAN
MARGARET ALBERTINA DIETER
RACHEL ELEANOR DONNELL
GRACE LILLIAN FILER
ELIZABETH WOODWORTH JAMESON
KATE KEITH
MARY FRANK KIMBALL
MARGARET ELIZABETH MILLER
MABEL LAINHART PARMELEE
JANE HOLMES PERKINS
LAURA KEZIAH PETTINGELL
ESTHER FRANCES PORTER
BESSIE KNIGHT ROBERTS
JANET SIMON
ELIZABETH ALLEN SMART
MARY ANNE STAPLES
KATHERINE STEVENS
ELSIE IRWIN SWEENEY
MABEL VAN DEUSEN
ANNA LORAINE WASHBURN
MARION CECILE WEBSTER
ELAINE SHEFFIELD WHITMAN

Alpha Society

Senior Officers

First Semester

President, CAROLINE DOREMUS PARK
Editor, VIRGINIA CORYELL CRAVEN

Second Semester

President, DOROTHY WATERMAN
Editor, HENRIETTA SPERRY

Senior Members

RUTH BALDWIN
BERNICE BARBER
ELEANOR PERRY BENSON
GERTRUDE BURBANK CHANDLER
VIRGINIA CORYELL CRAVEN
HELEN CHARLOTTE DENMAN
LOUISE KNAPP GATES
MARY ELLEN GEESAMAN
IDA REBECCA HOLLIDAY
KATE KEITH
ANNIS KENDALL
KATHARINE KING
ELINOR HAVEN MEANS

MARGARET APPLETON MEANS
TEI NINOMIYA
JEAN RHEA O'DONNEL
CAROLINE DOREMUS PARK
MARION KEEP PATTON
MILDRED RUDD PERRY
JESSIE WELLS POST
WINIFRED BARBARA SMITH
HENRIETTA SPERRY
MARY HENRY STEEN
DOROTHY WATERMAN
ELIZABETH PLATT WILDS
EDITH HOLMES WILLETTS

Phi Kappa Psi Society

First Semester
President, HELEN BIGELOW
Editor, MARY ALLERTON KILBORNE

Second Semester
President, ELISE SHATTUCK MONTGOMERY
Editor, MARY FRANK KIMBALL

Senior Members

HELEN CLEMENTINA BATES
KATHERINE BENNETT
MILDRED ADIENE BERGEN
HELEN BIGELOW
KATHRINE BOWMAN
HELEN OSGOOD BRADLEY
HARRIET FREDERICA BUCKLEY
BRETA WILLIS CHILDS
MARGUERITE CRAY
MARGARET DAUCHY
ALICE FAIRBANKS DAY
KATHARINE VAN VALKENBURGH DREW

DOROTHY GLADYS INGLEHART
MARY ALLERTON KILBORNE
MARY FRANK KIMBALL
FRANCES SPECK LONEY
SALLY JANE MCMULLIN
WINIFRED CHRISTINA METCALF
MARGARET ELIZABETH MILLER
ELISE SHATTUCK MONTGOMERY
HELEN NEWELL
PHOEBE MAE PARRY
ESTHER ANNE SMITH
LOUISA GODDARD VAN WAGENEN

KATHARINE LELAND WHITIN

Honorary Member
ELLEN HENRIETTA SKINNER

(79)

Officers

Pres., GRACE LILLIAN FILER   *Sec.*, MARGARET ADAMS CUSHMAN
Vice-Pres., HELEN CHARLOTTE DENMAN   *Treas.*, GERTRUDE LUDLAM ROBINSON
Executive Member, MARGARET ELIZABETH MILLER

Senior Members

ELFRIEDE MARIE ACKERMANN	MARY FRANK KIMBALL
HELEN GERTRUDE ALLEN	HELEN CUSHMAN KING
MADELINE ROBINSON BALL	MARION BUCK LINCOLN
BERNICE BARBER	MARGARET ELIZABETH MILLER
ELSIE NORA BRILEY	TEI NINOMIYA
ESTHER CRANE	MABEL LAINHART PARMELEE
MARGARET ADAMS CUSHMAN	MARION KEEP PATTON
ELIZABETH CORDELIA DECKER	JANE HOLMES PERKINS
HELEN CHARLOTTE DENMAN	GERTRUDE LUDLAM ROBINSON
RACHEL ELEANOR DONNELL	MURIEL SEELEY
GRACE LILLIAN FILER	WINIFRED BARBARA SMITH
MARJORIE FRASER	MARY ANNE STAPLES
LOUISE KNAPP GATES	PORTIA MANSFIELD SWETT
MARION HOWLAND	MABEL VAN DEUSEN
ELIZABETH WOODWORTH JAMESON	MARION CECILE WEBSTER
KATE KEITH	MARJORIE WELLS

Honorary Member

JANET SIMON

(80)

BIOLOGICAL SOCIETY.

Senior Officers

President, EVELYN ISABEL CANNING

Vice-President, ANNE GARDNER PIGEON

Senior Executive, WILMA RIDGWAY

Senior Members

CHARLOTTE BARKLEY BURGESS
EVELYN ISABEL CANNING
BRETA WILLIS CHILDS
HELEN BRAY DE LONG
RACHAEL ELEANOR DONNELL
EDITH UPHAM GILL
ELIZABETH STONE GREGORY
ALICE MABEL HASEY
MAUD BERNICE HAMMOND
ANNETTE LADD HOYT

HELEN SWIFT JONES
PEARL EVELYN LE VEQUE
GLADYS ELLSWORTH MOULTON
MARY PETERSON
ANNE GARDNER PIGEON
OLIVE FAWCETT PYE
ANN ELIZABETH RAWLS
WILMA RIDGWAY
EVELYN LOUISE RYDER
ELIZABETH SKINNER

VIOLA MARVIN SULLIVAN

Honorary Member

ELLEN HENRIETTA SKINNER

(81)

Officers

Secretary, AGNES RUTH CARTER
Treasurer, GERTRUDE MARTHA BARRY

Executive Committee

Secretary, MARGARET ELIZABETH MILLER
Ex-officio, HELEN STURTEVANT GIFFORD

Senior Members

GERTRUDE MARTHA BARRY
MAUDE EDNA BUSHNELL
AGNES RUTH CARTER
PHEBE CARTER
RACHAEL ELEANOR DONNELL
HELEN STURTEVANT GIFFORD

ANNA MARIA GRIFFIN
MARGARET ELIZABETH MILLER
TEI NINOMIYA
OLIVE FAWCETT PYE
ALMA SOPHIA ROTHHOLZ
EVA CEDELIA TEBBETTS

Senior Officers

President, ESTHER MARGARET SMITH
Vice-President, FLORENCE ANTHINE GRANT

Senior Members

ELSIE NORA BRILEY

ELINOR GARRETSON BROWN

PHEBE CARTER

HELEN STURTEVANT GIFFORD

FLORENCE ANTHINE GRANT

ANNA MARIA GRIFFIN

JOSIE MAGDALENE GRIFFIN

VIRGINIA PEIRCE

MARGUERITE SCOTT

ESTHER MARGARET SMITH

KATHERINE STEVENS

MABEL VAN DEUSEN

Senior Officers

President, LESLIE LELAND
Secretary, MARY BUNCE BREWSTER
Treasurer, MILDRED LOUISE MACDONALD

Senior Members

HELEN ALCOTT
JANE BUCKINGHAM ARMSTRONG
WILMA C. BAKER
MARY BUNCE BREWSTER
GRACE CATHARINE BRIGGS
MARJORIE LATHROP BROWNING
CHARLOTTE BARKLEY BURGESS
EDITH NANCY CARSON
PHEBE CARTER
MIRIAM ELLIOT CLAY
EDITH COLEMAN

LOUISE HADLEY CURTIS
FLORENCE FULLER
ELIZABETH HIGGIE JACKSON
LESLIE LELAND
MILDRED LOUISE MACDONALD
ESTHER FRANCES PORTER
HELEN NEWTON REES
FRANCES ROE
EVA CEDELIA TEBBETTS
RUTH ELIZABETH TUTTLE
ELAINE SHEFFIELD WHITMAN

RUA LOUISE YEAW

Honorary Members

AGNES RUTH CARTER

KATHERINE STEVENS

Senior Officers

Vice-President, MARJORIE FRASER
Member Executive Committee, HELEN ALCOTT

Senior Members

HELEN ALCOTT
GERTRUDE MARTHA BARRY
MARJORIE LATHROP BROWNING
CHARLOTTE BARKLEY BURGESS
MARGUERITE CRAY
MARJORIE FRASER
ELIZABETH WOODWORTH JAMESON

HELEN JEFFERS
KATHERINE ELEANOR JENKINS
EDNA CHIPMAN MOEHRING
TEI NINOMIYA
ETHEL LOUISE NORTON
VIRGINIA PEIRCE
HELEN NEWTON REES

Senior Officers

President, KATHRINE BOWMAN
Vice-President, ALICE STEPHANIE O'MEARA

Senior Members

KATHERINE BENNETT
KATHRINE BOWMAN
ELISE LORD BRADFORD
ELOISE RUGGLES CHANDLER
ELIZABETH SHELDON DOW
ALICE BLANCHE JACOT
RUTH LEIGHTON
ALICE STEPHANIE O'MEARA
EDITH MAGDALENE MANNING

MARGARET MARION PARK
PHOEBE MAE PARRY
EDITH CAROLINE RIKER
MURIEL SEELEY
JANET SIMON
FRANCES PIERPONT SIVITER
ETHEL STIMSON
MARION ELSIE WILMOT
GERTRUDE ELIZABETH WILSON

Honorary Members

RUTH BALDWIN
VIRGINIA CORYELL CRAVEN
HELEN CHARLOTTE DENMAN
JUANITA EMILY FIELD

KATHARINE VAN VALKENBURGH DREW
MARGARET ELIZABETH MILLER
MARION KEEP PATTON
GERTRUDE LUDLAM ROBINSON

(86)

Senior Officers

First Semester

President, BERNICE BARBER
Vice-President, MARY BLANCHARD SCOTT

Second Semester

President, ALICE STEPHANIE O'MEARA
Vice-President, CLARA EVA VAN EMDEN

Senior Members

ELFRIEDE MARIE ACKERMANN
ALICE WARDELL BAKER
BERNICE BARBER
MARTHA BARKER
MARGARET ALBERTINA DIETER
HELEN ELMA HEMPHILL
HELEN CUSHMAN KING
MARGARETTA NORRIS
ALICE STEPHANIE O'MEARA
MABEL LAINHART PARMELEE

RUTH SHATTUCK PERKINS
ANN ELIZABETH RAWLS
ALMA SOPHIA ROTHHOLZ
ALMA CARROL SCHLESINGER
MARY BLANCHARD SCOTT
ESTHER MARGARET SMITH
CLARA EVA VAN EMDEN
MARJORIE WELLS
EDNAH AUGUSTA WHITNEY
ETHEL SOMERS WILSON

Honorary Member

HARRIET FREDERICA BUCKLEY

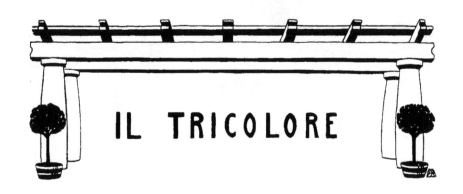

IL TRICOLORE

Senior Officers

President, HELEN NEWTON REES
Secretary, MARY ANNE STAPLES
Treasurer, EVA BARNS

Senior Members

LOUISE MORSE BAILEY

EVA BARNS

MARY BUNCE BREWSTER

MARGUERITE CRAY

JUANITA EMILY FIELD

IRENE EMMA HOYT

ELIZABETH WOODWORTH JAMESON

RUTH HOBBY MITCHELL

FLORENCE GRACE MURRAY

HELEN NEWTON REES

MARGUERITE SCOTT

MARY ANNE STAPLES

ELIZABETH ALLEN STUART

MARION THOMAS

Honorary Members

ETHEL RAE DUGAN

CHRISTINE ALEXANDER GRAHAM

GERTRUDE VALÉRIE MCCLINTOCK

EL CLUB ESPAÑOL

Senior Officers

Vice-President, FRANCES ROE
Secretary and Treasurer, ANNA LORAINE WASHBURN

Senior Members

HELEN GERTRUDE ALLEN

LOUISE MORSE BAILEY

ANNA ELIZABETH BLODGETT

BERTHA BODINE

LOUISE HADLEY CURTIS

FLORENCE ANTHINE GRANT

FRANCES ROE

ELIZABETH ALLEN SMART

ANNA LORAINE WASHBURN

Honorary Members

GRACE CAROLINE ALLING

ELEANOR PERRY BENSON

ESTHER ANN SMITH

Senior Officers

First Semester

Chairman Executive Committee
HELEN GERTRUDE ALLEN

Secretary and Treasurer
LOUISE HADLEY CURTIS

Senior Member Executive Committee
MARION CECILE WEBSTER

Second Semester

Chairman Executive Committee
LAURA KEZIAH PETTINGELL

Senior Member Executive Committee
JANE HOLMES PERKINS

Senior Members

HELEN GERTRUDE ALLEN	SALLY JANE MCMULLIN
EDITH COLEMAN	JANE HOLMES PERKINS
LOUISE HADLEY CURTIS	LAURA KEZIAH PETTINGELL
MARGARET ALBERTINA DIETER	ONA EMILY PFLUKE
MARGARET ALINE FELLOWS	ELIZABETH ALLEN SMART
ALICE GARDNER HOWE	GLADYS REMSEN VAN DEVENTER
MARY ETTA LOUISE MARTIN	MARION CECILE WEBSTER

MILDRED CLAIRE WILLIAMS

Honorary Member

ELLEN HENRIETTA SKINNER

Senior Officers

President, ELIZABETH CURTIS WRIGHT
Secretary, MARJORIE WELLS

Senior Members

GRACE CATHARINE BRIGGS
EDITH COLEMAN
MARGARET ALBERTINA DIETER
ANNE GARNETT
MARGARET LORING GILBERT
HARRIET HELOISE HEDGES
DOROTHY GLADYS INGLEHART
FRANCES ADELAIDE JOHNSTONE
GLADYS MENDUM
WINIFRED CHRISTINA L. METCALF
TEI NINOMIYA

AZALIA EMMA PEET
JANE HOLMES PERKINS
RUTH SHATTUCK PERKINS
ANNE GARDNER PIGEON
JESSIE LEE RIALL
ANNA EMILY SIGAFUS
YEOLI STIMSON
VIOLA MARVIN SULLIVAN
FLORENCE WARD
MARJORIE WELLS
ELIZABETH CURTIS WRIGHT

Honorary Member

HARRIET FREDERICA BUCKLEY

Senior Officer

President, ANNETTE LADD HOYT

Senior Members

NORMA MACLEOD ANDERSON

FRANCESCA BARTLETT

ELSIE NORA BRILEY

IDA REBECCA HOLLIDAY

ANNETTE LADD HOYT

FRANCES SPECK LONEY

FRANCES JOSEPHA E. MANN

LOUISE ESTELLE MARDEN

GERTRUDE VALÉRIE MCCLINTOCK

ALDANA RIPLEY QUIMBY

WILMA RIDGWAY

MARTHA ERMINIE ROST

ESTHER ANN SMITH

PORTIA MANSFIELD SWETT

LOUISA GODDARD VAN WAGENEN

JULIET ESTELLE VALENTINE

MARJORIE VALENTINE

MARION CECILE WEBSTER

Honorary Member

PHOEBE MAE PARRY

PIANO

Clef Club

Officer

President, MABEL LAINHART PARMELEE

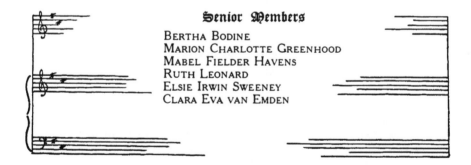

Senior Members

BERTHA BODINE
MARION CHARLOTTE GREENHOOD
MABEL FIELDER HAVENS
RUTH LEONARD
ELSIE IRWIN SWEENEY
CLARA EVA VAN EMDEN

Senior Officers

First Semester
PEARL EVELYN LE VEQUE

Second Semester
HILDA MARY CAMP

Senior Members

ELISE LORD BRADFORD
HILDA MARY CAMP
ANNIS KENDALL

PEARL EVELYN LE VEQUE
ALICE BROWNE McGUIRE
MARGARET APPLETON MEANS

MARY HENRY STEEN

Ex-Member
ETHEL SOMERS WILSON

Officer

President, KATHARINE LELAND WHITIN

Senior Members

MARY ALEXANDER

VIRGINIA CORYELL CRAVEN

IDA REBECCA HOLLIDAY

JOSEPHINE KEIZER

KATHARINE KING

SALLY JANE MCMULLIN

MARGARET APPLETON MEANS

CAROLINE DOREMUS PARK

ALMA CARROL SCHLESINGER

DOROTHY WATERMAN

KATHARINE LELAND WHITIN

ELIZABETH PLATT WILDS

Officer

President, JUANITA EMILY FIELD

Senior Members

BERNICE BARBER

MILDRED ADIENE BERGEN

HELEN BIGELOW

MARION ELIZABETH BOOTH

MARGUERITE CRAY

MARGARET DAUCHY

JUANITA EMILY FIELD

PHOEBE MAE PARRY

JESSIE WELLS POST

ESTHER ANN SMITH

JULIET ESTELLE VALENTINE

EDITH HOLMES WILLETTS

1908=1909
President, GERTRUDE ELIZABETH WILSON

1909=1910
President, MARION KEEP PATTON

Members

MILDRED SIDNEY BALDWIN
CAROLINE STINSON BURNE
ESTHER CRANE
VIRGINIA CORYELL CRAVEN
JOSEPHINE KEIZER
MARY ALLERTON KILBORNE
MARY FRANK KIMBALL
MARY ELIZABETH LUCE
GRACE BROWNE McGUIRE
MARGARET APPLETON MEANS

HELENA FRANKLIN MILLER
ALICE STEPHANIE O'MEARA
MARION KEEP PATTON
PHOEBE MAE PARRY
ANNABEL HITCHCOCK SHARP
JANET SIMON
HENRIETTA SPERRY
JESSIE LAUREL SULLIVAN
MARJORIE TALBOT
MILDRED CLAIRE WILLIAMS

GERTRUDE ELIZABETH WILSON

NOVEL CLUB

Officers

President, VIOLA MARVIN SULLIVAN

Vice-President, ELIZABETH PLATT WILDS

Members

MILDRED ADIENE BERGEN

CAROLINE STINSON BURNE

VIRGINIA CORYELL CRAVEN

MARGARET DAUCHY

ANNA FINKBINE

LOUISE KNAPP GATES

FANNY VOSE HAZEN

IDA REBECCA HOLLIDAY

DOROTHY GLADYS INGLEHART

KATHARINE KING

MARGARET APPLETON MEANS

WINIFRED BARBARA SMITH

LOUISA GODDARD VAN WAGENEN

KATHARINE LELAND WHITIN

GRANDDAUGHTERS' SOCIETY

Officer

President, FLORENCE FREELAND CURTIS

Senior Members

FLORENCE FREELAND CURTIS   HARRIET HELOISE HEDGES

ANNA LORAINE WASHBURN

Sanior Officers

Chafe Cooke, ESSIE O'SMITH
Walkin' Diligate, KATIE O'KING

Sanior Mimbers

IDY McANDRUS

BRANIE O'BARBER

KATIE O'DREW

MAMIE O'GEESAMAN

KATIE O'KING

JISSIE O'LEWIS

FANNIE O'LONEY

LIZZIE O'MONTGOMERY

PETIE O'NEWELL

ESSIE O'SMITH

WINNIE O'SMITH

EDIE O'WILLETTS

Orangemen

Senior Officers

The Great High O'ZOMORON O *Zophostovoto*
IDA HOLLIDAY
O Kerachoratumeri Tsorjorarum
ELIZABETH WILDS
The Lord High Caradoto of Order
MARY ALEXANDER

Senior Members

Orizido MARY ALEXANDER
Orizido RUTH BALDWIN
Orizido ELEANOR BENSON
Orizido HELEN BIGELOW
Orizido MARGARET DAUCHY
Orizido LOUISE GATES

Orizido IDA HOLLIDAY
Orizido JEAN O'DONNEL
Orizido CAROLINE PARK
Orizido MARY SCOTT
Orizido DOROTHY WATERMAN
Orizido KATHARINE WHITIN

Orizido ELIZABETH WILDS

Officers

1908—1909
President, HELEN NEWELL

1909—1910
President, MARY ALEXANDER

Members

MARY ALEXANDER
GERTRUDE CHANDLER
BRETA CHILDS
LOUISE GATES
MARY GEESAMAN
IDA HOLLIDAY
KATHARINE KING
JESSICA LEWIS

FRANCES LONEY
ELISE MONTGOMERY
HELEN NEWELL
JEAN O'DONNEL
CAROLINE PARK
EDITH RIKER
WINIFRED SMITH
DOROTHY WATERMAN

KATHARINE WHITIN

Honorary Members

GRACE ROSE   HILDA TALMAGE

Officer

Constellation-in-Chief, MARS SMITH

Members

CAPRICORN BROWNING

SATURN GEESAMAN

CASTOR JOHNSTON

SHOOTING-STAR LEWIS

CASSIOPE-AND-CHAIR LONEY

POLLUX MARDEN

LITTLE DIPPER PARK

EVENING STAR WATERMAN

TWINKLE-TWINKLE WHITIN

URANUS WILDS

MERCURY WILLETTS

SOPHOMORE YEAR

An epic of an epoch grand
  Historic Muse begin to write.
You ask what class? You ask what year?
  "One wouldn't think that you were bright."

That fall when hand clasped hand of her
  She didn't know by sight last year,
Remember when we said to each
  "How great to see you back, my dear!"?
Remember how we climbed the hill,
  Our love for each old spot confessing?
Remember on our suitcase boy
  How we bestowed both coin and blessing?
Remember when he went with haste
  To get another tip he joyed in
How, weeping tears of purest joy,
  We fell on soup and Mrs. Boyden?
Remember?—but I need not ask;
  Fond mem'ries like the scent of jasmine,
Rush back to sweeten later years,
  What else could rhyme with second classmen!
Class meeting came—we met in state—
  That is, in Room 10, Seelye.
With training gained from Freshman year
  We spoke our minds quite freely.
Our president was Mary A,
  We're glad we made the motion;
For now we're sure that no one could
  Have served with more devotion.

But what we really came here for—
  (According to our teachers),
The discipline of life was felt
  As well as pleasant features.
On orange cards we wrote our names
  —'Twas all we could enlarge in—
For lo! the course we should pursue
  Already in the margin.
When requirement and election
  In this happy year did clash.
Requirement being very strong,
  Election went to smash.
Miss Billings and Miss Jocelyn
  With patience quite invincible,
Stood by us on the inclined plane
  And Archimedes Principle.

(104)

While those who chose the substitute,
    Beside their morning classes,
Spent sad p. m.'s in chemic Lab
    Midst horrid-smelling gases.
For us the Bible course was changed,
    —Nice syllabi no longer—
Despite our prayers to Grant them still,
    They Wood give something stronger!
$2.00 for a fat green book
    We never hoped to sell,
About the minor prophets
    And Isaiah much did tell.
This all led up to English B.
    Alas! but few succeeded
In writing on her chosen theme
    Quite all the subject needed.
But, even then, we all got through,
    Our knowledge was a factor,
Though all our papers plainly showed
    The hand of the Redactor.

B also stood for Basket Ball,
    Big Game and Much Ado,
D. Waterman said "do your best";
    We did the Odds up too.
B also stood for Burton
    Who addressed us on that day,
And on his chosen subject,
    Had quite a bit to say.

Yet long before that Rally Day
    Full many were the gists,
And for first five and many more
    We handed in our lists.
We trailed for Alpha—then, oh joy!
    Soon after came Phi Kap;
Gifts for our little mates took in
    Allowances did sap.
We'd like to go in all the clubs
    Now we are eligible.
But we must pass the office first,
    And meet full many a quibble.
The camel can more easy far
    Pass through the eye of needle
Than dunces can that office pass
    By diplomatic wheedle.
Our feet inclined to devious ways,
    Were clad in shoes æsthetic;
And surely 'twas a comic sight
    Had it not been pathetic

To see us pirouette and slide
  Quite from a sense of duty,
Miss Eisenbrey adjuring us
  To step with grace and beauty.

The French club gave a witty play
  And some of us were in it,
But that we understood it all
  Don't think it for a minute.
We went to see Maude Adams
  In a rain that was quite drenchin'
And wore our rubber coats, which soon
  The New York papers mention.
But, speaking of dramatics
  We preferred the Vaudeville.
From ten cent seats we saw such feats
  As linger with us still.

From "spring recess" we all returned
  With joy and "Merry widows,"
The town was over-roofed with us
  And those enormous liddos.
We crowd the transepts very full
  In hearts not hats united,
Yet sometimes under one of these
  A once-loved friend was sighted.

Spring term ensued with all its joys
  As in the years gone by,
But from our tender Sophomore breasts
  It wrung the heavy sigh;
Not all because we had to say
  Good-bye to gym forever,
But since from dearest 1908
  We must so shortly sever.
Last teas, last bats about the green,
  Last sings upon the campus,
Nor all the equinoctial gales
  Could yet suffice to damp us.

Then good-bye to the Pretenders
  Which moved us all to tears,
Good-bye to our dear sister class,
  And to the best of years.

           VIRGINIA CORYELL CRAVEN.

President of the Council
MILDRED RUDD PERRY

(107)

Smith College Council

Senior Councillors

HELEN BIGELOW   CAROLINE DOREMUS PARK

MARY ALLERTON KILBORNE   MILDRED RUDD PERRY

Junior Councillors

HELEN BIGELOW   MARY ALLERTON KILBORNE

MILDRED RUDD PERRY

Sophomore Councillors

KATHRINE BOWMAN   MARY ALLERTON KILBORNE

Freshman Councillor

KATHRINE BOWMAN

S. C. A. C. W.

Senior Officers

President, DOROTHY GLADYS INGLEHART
Vice-President, KATE KEITH

Missionary Department

Chairman, RUTH SHATTUCK PERKINS
Chairman Mission Study Committee, HELEN CHARLOTTE DENMAN

Membership Committee
Chairman, KATE KEITH

Religious Service Committee
Chairman, HENRIETTA SPERRY

Bible Study Committee
Chairman, VIOLA MARVIN SULLIVAN

Home Culture Club Committee
Chairman, GRACE CATHARINE BRIGGS

Social Committee
Chairman, MILDRED RUDD PERRY

Consumers' League Committee
Chairman, FANNY VOSE HAZEN

Junior Officers
Recording Secretary, HELEN CHARLOTTE DENMAN
Corresponding Secretary, MARY ALEXANDER
Chairman Students' Exchange, SALLY JANE MCMULLIN
Chairman Finance Committee, DOROTHY WATERMAN
Chairman Extension Committee, KATE KEITH
Elector College Settlement Chapter, HELEN OSGOOD BRADLEY

Sophomore Officers
Treasurer, HENRIETTA SPERRY
Assistant Treasurer, ETHEL SOMERS WILSON

Freshman Representatives
WINIFRED CHRISTINA L. MELCALF   MARJORIE VALENTINE

PUBLICATIONS

The Monthly Board

Editor-in-Chief
MARY FRANK KIMBALL*   JOSEPHINE KEIZER

Literary Editor
MARGARET APPLETON MEANS

Sketch Editor
KATHARINE DUNCAN MORSE*   HELENA FRANKLIN MILLER

Editor's Table
MARION KEEP PATTON

Managing Editors
ANNABEL HITCHCOCK SHARP*   ALICE STEPHANIE O'MEARA
PHOEBE MAE PARRY

Assistant Managing Editor   *Alumnae Editor*
ESTHER CRANE   JESSIE LAUREL SULLIVAN

About College Editor
VIRGINIA CORYELL CRAVEN

Treasurer   *Alumnae Treasurer*
GERTRUDE ELIZABETH WILSON   HENRIETTA SPERRY

Business Manager
MILDRED SIDNEY BALDWIN

*Resigned.

(112)

Officer

President, ALICE FAIRBANKS DAY

Senior Member

VIRGINIA CORYELL CRAVEN

Honorary Members

KATE KEITH   MARGARET APPLETON MEANS

HENRIETTA SPERRY

The Class Book Board

Manager, JUANITA EMILY FIELD

Assistant Manager, LOUISE KNAPP GATES

Drawings, PEARL EVELYN LE VEQUE

Literary, PHOEBE MAE PARRY

Assistant Literary, EDITH UPHAM GILL

Photographs, HELEN OSGOOD BRADLEY

Business Manager, ELOISE RUGGLES CHANDLER

Freshman Basketball Team

Freshman Basketball Team

Captain, DOROTHY WATERMAN

Homes
RUTH BALDWIN
IDA REBECCA HOLLIDAY
EDITH CAROLINE RIKER

Centers
ANNETTE LADD HOYT
ELINOR HAVEN MEANS
CAROLYN LOUISE SHAW

Guards
KATHARINE CLARK BROWNING   MARION CHARLOTTE GREENHOOD
DOROTHY WATERMAN

1909 vs. 1910

Saturday, March 16, 1907

Score: 31—16

Freshman Substitute Basketball Team

Captain, MARGARET DAUCHY

Homes
HELEN CLEMENTINA BATES
MARGARET DAUCHY
HILDA TALMAGE

Centers
NORMA MACLEOD ANDERSON
IRMA LOIS MILLER
ALMA SOPHIA ROTHHOLZ

Guards
DOROTHY AVERILL   ELEANOR PERRY BENSON
PHOEBE MAE PARRY

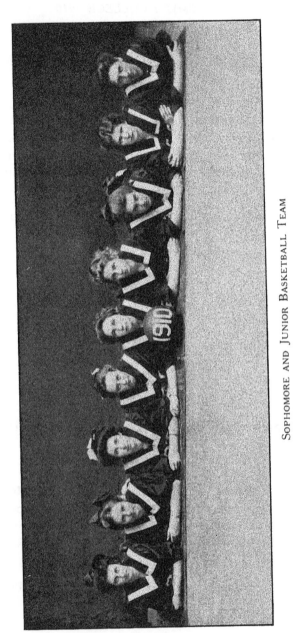

SOPHOMORE AND JUNIOR BASKETBALL TEAM

Sophomore and Junior Basketball Team

Captain, DOROTHY WATERMAN

Homes
IDA REBECCA HOLLIDAY
ELINOR HAVEN MEANS
EDITH CAROLINE RIKER

Centers
ANNETTE LADD HOYT
JEAN RHEA O'DONNEL
CAROLYN LOUISE SHAW

Guards
RUTH BALDWIN   MARION CHARLOTTE GREENHOOD
DOROTHY WATERMAN

1910 vs. 1911

Saturday, March 7, 1908

Score: 38—18

Sophomore and Junior Substitute Basketball Team

Captain, MARGARET DAUCHY

Homes
HELEN CLEMENTINA BATES
MARGARET DAUCHY
FRANCES JOSEPHA EDDY MANN

Centers
NORMA MACLEOD ANDERSON
IRMA LOIS MILLER
ALMA SOPHIA ROTHHOLZ

Guards
ELEANOR PERRY BENSON   KATHARINE CLARK BROWNING
PHOEBE MAE PARRY

Senior Basketball Team

Captain, JEAN RHEA O'DONNEL

Homes

IDA REBECCA HOLLIDAY

ELINOR HAVEN MEANS

EDITH CAROLINE RIKER

Centers

ANNETTE LADD HOYT

JEAN RHEA O'DONNEL

CAROLYN LOUISE SHAW

Guards

RUTH BALDWIN

MARION CHARLOTTE GREENHOOD

PHOEBE MAE PARRY

Senior Substitute Basketball Team

Captain, MARGARET DAUCHY

Homes

MILDRED ADIENE BERGEN

MARGARET DAUCHY

FRANCES JOSEPHA EDDY MANN

Centers

NORMA MACLEOD ANDERSON

EDITH MAGDALENE MANNING

ALMA SOPHIA ROTHHOLZ

Guards

ELEANOR PERRY BENSON

OPAL MAY BRACKEN

MARY GRUMMAN WINANS

Hockey Team

Captain, ELISE SHATTUCK MONTGOMERY

Forwards

OPAL MAY BRACKEN
ALICE FAIRBANKS DAY
      MILDRED SAWYER

ANNETTE LADD HOYT
PHOEBE MAE PARRY

Half-Backs

ELISE SHATTUCK MONTGOMERY   ARDRA SOULE
      MARY GRUMMAN WINANS

Full-Backs

MURIEL JOHNSTON   PORTIA MANSFIELD SWETT

Goal

KATHARINE CLARK BROWNING

Cricket Team

Captain, MARGUERITE SCOTT

Senior Members

RUTH BALDWIN

ELEANOR PERRY BENSON

OPAL MAY BRACKEN

ELINOR HAVEN MEANS

JEAN RHEA O'DONNEL

PHOEBE MAE PARRY

EMELIE MUNSON PERKINS

MARGUERITE SCOTT

CAROLINE LOUISE SHORE

PORTIA MANSFIELD SWETT

MARY GRUMMAN WINANS

Substitute Team

MARY ALEXANDER

MURIEL JOHNSTON

ARDRA SOULE

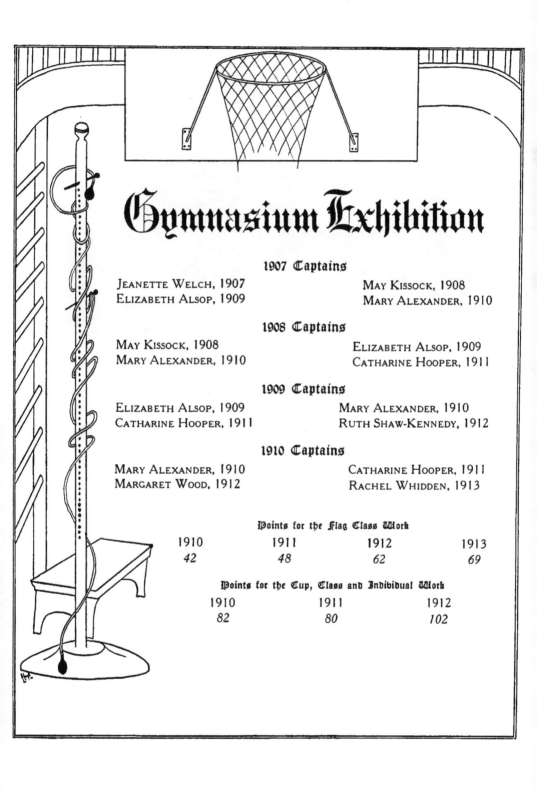

Gymnasium Exhibition

1907 Captains

JEANETTE WELCH, 1907   MAY KISSOCK, 1908
ELIZABETH ALSOP, 1909   MARY ALEXANDER, 1910

1908 Captains

MAY KISSOCK, 1908   ELIZABETH ALSOP, 1909
MARY ALEXANDER, 1910   CATHARINE HOOPER, 1911

1909 Captains

ELIZABETH ALSOP, 1909   MARY ALEXANDER, 1910
CATHARINE HOOPER, 1911   RUTH SHAW-KENNEDY, 1912

1910 Captains

MARY ALEXANDER, 1910   CATHARINE HOOPER, 1911
MARGARET WOOD, 1912   RACHEL WHIDDEN, 1913

Points for the Flag Class Work

1910	1911	1912	1913
42	48	62	69

Points for the Cup, Class and Individual Work

1910	1911	1912
82	80	102

ALLEN FIELD CLUB HOUSE

Officers from 1910

Freshman Year

Representative, EDITH CAROLINE RIKER

Sophomore Year

Secretary, CAROLINE DOREMUS PARK
Treasurer, WINIFRED CHRISTINA L. METCALF
Representative, RUTH BALDWIN

Junior Year

President, WINIFRED CHRISTINA L. METCALF
Representative, CAROLINE DOREMUS PARK
Chairman Tennis Committee, FRANCES ADELAIDE JOHNSTONE
Chairman Sandwich Committee, EDITH HOLMES WILLETTS

Senior Year

Vice-President, WINIFRED CHRISTINA L. METCALF
Representative, PHOEBE MAE PARRY
Chairman of the Club-house Committee, EDITH HOLMES WILLETTS

Tennis Championships

1907

Singles	Ruth Cowing, 1907
Doubles	{ Eva Baker, 1907 { Ruth Cowing, 1907

1908

Singles	Winifred Notman, 1911
Doubles	{ Sara Evans, 1911 { Winifred Notman, 1911

1909

Singles	Nan Martin, 1912
Doubles	{ Elizabeth Bryan, 1909 { Ruth Henley, 1909

Field Day
May 15, 1909

Field Day Spectators

GAME	POINTS		PLAYERS	WINNER
Hockey	5 for winner	3 for loser	..................1909-1910....................	.1909
Basketball	5 for winner	3 for loser	..................1909-1910....................	.1910
Archery	4 for winner	2 for loser	..................1911-1912....................	.1912
Cricket	4 for winner	2 for loser	..................1910-1911....................	.1910

Tennis Finals

(126)

Volley Ball

GAME	POINTS	PLAYERS	WINNER
Croquet	3 for winner / 1 for loser	1909-1910	1910
Tennis	5 for winner / 3 for loser	1909-1912	1909
Volley Ball	4 for winner / 2 for loser	1912-1911	1911
Clock Golf	3 for winner / 1 for loser	1910-1911	1910

Basketball

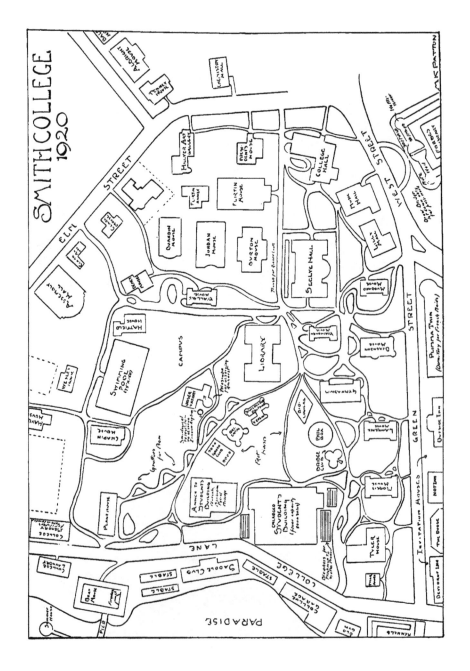

SMITH COLLEGE 1920

MUSICAL CLUBS

GLEE CLUB

Glee Club

Leader, CARRIE DELLA WRIGHT, 1910
Assistant Leader, MABEL FIELDER HAVENS, 1910
Manager, HELEN CHARLOTTE DENMAN, 1910
Treasurer, HAZEL GLEASON, 1911
Accompanist, ELSIE IRWIN SWEENEY, 1910

First Sopranos

MARGUERITE E. BRUMAGHIM, 1910
HELEN CHARLOTTE DENMAN, 1910
FLORENCE ELIZABETH HOPWOOD, 1910
EDITH HOLMES WILLETTS, 1910
HAZEL GLEASON, 1911
DORIS LOUISE NASH, 1911
REBECCA ELMER SMITH, 1911
MARGARET HENSLEY WOODBRIDGE, 1911
GRACE MAY HOFFMAN, 1912
RUTH HARRIET LEWIN, 1912
LOUISA FRANCES SPEAR, 1912
RUTH ANNIE WOOD, 1912

Second Sopranos

KATHERINE BENNETT, 1910
LOUISE ESTELLE MARDEN, 1910
WINIFRED CHRISTINA L. METCALF 1910
MARGARET THOMPSON BURLEIGH, 1911
ELSA DETMOLD, 1911
EDITH LOBDELL, 1911
GERTRUDE WELLS LYFORD, 1911
MARGARET MCCRARY, 1911
BERTHA JANE WARD, 1911
MARIE COUWENHOVEN BASSETT, 1912
MARION DENMAN, 1912
RHEA MARGUERITE PATON, 1912

First Altos

MAUDE LINES HAMILTON, 1910
ARLINE GREENLEE BROOKS, 1911
HELEN AUGUSTA BROWN, 1911
ANNAH PARKMAN BUTLER, 1911
LOUISE ASHLEY WEST, 1911
LAURA ELIZABETH WILBER, 1911
EUGENIE VALESKA FINK, 1912

Second Altos

RUTH BALDWIN, 1910
MABEL FIELDER HAVENS, 1910
MYRTLE IRENE ALDERMAN, 1911
MILDRED CAREY, 1912
RUTH EVANS, 1912
HELEN MENZIES NORTHRUP, 1912

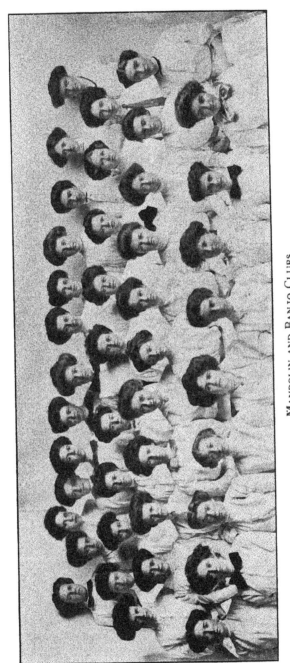

Mandolin and Banjo Clubs

Mandolin Club

Leader, PORTIA MANSFIELD SWETT, 1910
Manager, CAROLYN WOOLLEY, 1911

First Mandolins

ELEANOR PERRY BENSON, 1910
MARION AUGUSTA CROZIER, 1910
ETHEL RAE DUGAN, 1910
MARJORIE FRASER, 1910
HELEN STURTEVANT GIFFORD, 1910
MARION CHARLOTTE GREENHOOD, 1910

EDITHA MINER, 1910
MILDRED SAWYER, 1910
PORTIA MANSFIELD SWETT, 1910
ADALINE BELL MOYER, 1911
DORIS PATTERSON, 1911
CAROLYN WOOLLEY, 1911

Second Mandolins

EDNAH AUGUSTA WHITNEY, 1910
JOSEPHINE HANNAH DOLE, 1912

MADALENE FAY DOW, 1912
HENRIETTA CHANDLER PEABODY, 1912

Third Mandolins

ANNETTE LADD HOYT, 1910
BERTHA LOUISE SKINNER, 1910

MARION STEWART DITMAN, 1911
EDITH LOUISE WILLIAMS, 1912

Guitars

IRENE EMMA HOYT, 1910
ANNA LORAINE WASHBURN, 1910
GERTRUDE RUSSELL, 1911

RUTH JOSLIN, 1912
MARY PARMLY KOUES, 1912
DOROTHY MURISON, 1912

Violins

MARY LIVINGSTON RICE, 1911
DOROTHY STODDARD, 1912
MILDRED FRANCES WEBSTER, 1912

Violoncellos

ESTHER MARGARET SMITH, 1910
KATHARINE LOIS OTIS, 1912

Properties

MURIEL JOHNSTON, 1910

Banjo Club

Leader, IDA BOURNE ANDRUS, 1910
Manager, KATHERINE SCHUYLER HUBBS, 1910

Banjeaurines

IDA BOURNE ANDRUS, 1910

CHRISTINE ALEXANDER GRAHAM, 1910

KATHERINE SCHUYLER HUBBS, 1910

ALENE AYRES, 1912

MARION ELIZABETH CLARK, 1912

EDITH FITZGERALD, 1912

ELOISE HARVEY, 1912

Banjos

FLORENCE ANTHINE GRANT, 1910

FRANCES ADELAIDE JOHNSTONE, 1910

MARTHA ERMINIE ROST, 1910

MARY ANNE STAPLES, 1910

RUTH ELIZABETH TUTTLE, 1910

Guitars

MARY PETERSON, 1910

ANN ELIZABETH RAWLS, 1910

Properties

MURIEL JOHNSTON, 1910

Choir and Orchestra

College Orchestra

Leader, Louisa Goddard Van Wagenen

Senior Members

Ida Bourne Andrus
Marjorie Elliott Simmons
Esther Margaret Smith
Louisa Goddard Van Wagenen
Marjorie Wells

Chapel Choir

Assistant Leader, Alice Stephanie O'Meara

Senior Members

Ethel Benedict Ayres
Alice Wardell Baker
Ruth Baldwin
Anna Elizabeth Blodgett
Marguerite Brumaghim
Gertrude Chapin
Elizabeth Cordelia Decker
Maude Lines Hamilton
Mabel Fielder Havens
Florence Elizabeth Hopwood
Effie Marguérite Kelso
Mary Margaret Kneeland

Edith Collin Lawrence
Gertrude Ethel Milham
Margaret Marion Park
Marion Keep Patton
Mary Louise Reilly
Edna Alice Roberts
Bertha Louise Skinner
Ardra Soule
Henrietta Sperry
Clara Eva Van Emden
Edith Holmes Willetts
Marion Elsie Wilmot

Carrie Della Wright

MISS JORDAN AND MR. SLEEPER

MR. PIERCE AND MR. HADZSITS

MR. HILDT

MISS EASTMAN

JUNIOR YEAR

September of Junior year found us quite prepared to take our place as upper classmen. Optimism and progress were our watchwords. While still retaining unbounded admiration for our Alma Mater, we were no longer awed in the contemplation of her greatness. We found opportunities for improvement and we made the most of them. Yet so far as the calendar is concerned, we were quite Bromidic.

Our third Mountain Day was not essentially different from our other two. At Thanksgiving time those of us who did not find it convenient to spend the day in the midst of our adoring families, went to the gym and there witnessed the shameful victory of the Indians over the Puritans (35-17). We hope this was not symbolical of a changed emphasis in the observance of the day. Christmas vacation and mid-years, that bitter-sweet combination, and then came Rally Day. With more enthusiasm and joy than ever before, we filed into chapel in the morning. For one of our number, Marion Patton, was to deliver the Washington Ode. Needless to say, our expectations were splendidly fulfilled. Later, we went to the gym, the Seniors sang the usual topical song to all the classes and reminded us especially that "in September we'd remember 1909." Did ever a Junior class have such a frolic as we? And this in spite of vexations, cautions and admonitions from the office. In vain we sighed, "If all the world and the faculty were as innocent as we!" However, we attended the Mardi Gras in high spirits and Billikens, the benign god of things as they ought to be, presided over our festivities. The crowning of the Queen,—a superb creature, the Wild Man of Borneo, a refined vaudeville and moving picture show were leading events of the evening. Prom time found us (those who had secured men) equipped with dainty gowns, soft voices and witching smiles. Nor was the only man dance of our college course a failure. In spring term, with its bacon bats and sings, came Field Day. Of course it was very hot, but the even classes starred alike in basketball and croquet and we sang the dear old songs and ate strawberries and ice cream under the green trees in gladness of heart. Commencement time was so full of hurry and good-byes and struggling under the Ivy Chain that we simply couldn't think and so we decided to wait until another year to realize the meaning of it all.

And now for our improvements and reforms. In these our interest was, from the first, vivid and consuming. As the natural guardians of the incoming 1912 we nipped all lacrimose tendencies in the bud, and sought to foster in our sister class a spirit of independence and cheerfulness. In this laudable endeavor, Nature co-operated with us., The opening weeks of college were bright and sunshiny, without the usual drizzle and the customary Freshman rains.

We next turned our attention to the buildings. Under our auspices Baldwin House and Clark House were opened. The continued fair weather was favorable for laying the foundations of the new library, and by December much of the iron framework of the stacks, as well as the outside walls of brick and stone, was well under way. How we longed to inspect the building at close range! But the many signs, "No trespassing inside," restrained us. So from a safe distance and quite oblivious of the incessant hammering and of the men and carts and yellow clay and mud, we viewed the growing edifice. We forgot all about the crowding and confusion of the old reference library and dreamed dreams of luxurious, long, oak tables where we could browse away mid "the still air of delightful studies." In order not to obstruct the approach to the new library, it was necessary to move the Hatfield House and the old gym. For the latter, especially, this was a slow and laborious process. So slow was it that there were times when we almost despaired of its accomplishment. The advance was hardly perceptible from one day to the next. But our courage was high and meanwhile we selected the site and approved the plans for the new auditorium.

Our activities, however, were not limited to improvements in the campus and buildings. It is to 1910 that future classes will look back as the originators of the system whereby a demerit is the penalty for lateness in handing in exercise cards. The careless, negligent habits of former classes were no longer to be tolerated. Still further in the interests of precision and incidentally at the suggestion of the alumnæ, we secured the printing and distribution of the rules and regulations under which we live.

Finally, owing to President Seelye's definitive resignation, we were obliged to select a new president. This was the most difficult task of our Junior year. How we did worry our little heads over it all, discussing now this person and now that. But finally our minds were decided. The trustees assured us that we had made no mistake.

In view of this unflagging zeal which we have never failed to manifest for our Alma Mater, who can doubt that 1910 itself will ere long be represented on the board of trustees and through them continue the good work begun here?

MARY FRANK KIMBALL

Committee

Chairman, MARGARET DAUCHY

ELEANOR PERRY BENSON   GRACE BROWNE MCGUIRE

FANNY VOSE HAZEN   ELIZABETH PLATT WILDS

Mardi Gras

Procession

King and his Train . . . . TYLER HOUSE

Queen and her Train . . . . EVEN INN

Band . . . . HAVEN HOUSE

Dancing Dervishes . . . . MORRIS HOUSE

Foreign Ambassadors . . . . CHAPIN HOUSE

Side Shows

Restaurant with continual Vaudeville .... ALBRIGHT HOUSE

Advertisements .... WASHBURN HOUSE

Beauty Shop .... LAWRENCE HOUSE

Dance Hall .... HUBBARD HOUSE

Freaks .... WALLACE HOUSE

Fortune Telling Booths, Peanut and Pop- ⎧ DEWEY, TENNEY,
corn Venders, Country Bumpkins, ⎨ CLARK AND
Sightseers, Etc. .... ⎩ BALDWIN HOUSES

Vaudeville

Coon Songs .... ⎰ ARDRA SOULE
⎱ ANNE GARDNER PIGEON

Juggling .... TEI NINOMIYA

Moving Pictures .... DICKINSON HOUSE

Bowery Duet .... ⎰ LOUISE ESTELLE MARDEN
⎱ MURIEL JOHNSTON

Dancers .... ⎰ PORTIA MANSFIELD SWETT
⎱ ANNETTE LADD HOYT

Melodrama .... DEAD MEN'S GULCH

IDA REBECCA HOLLIDAY   LOUISA GODDARD VAN WAGENEN
GRACE BROWNE McGUIRE   ELIZABETH PLATT WILDS

Junior Promenade

May 12, 1909

Committees

General Chairman, KATHERINE BENNETT

Floor

Chairman, GERTRUDE WILSON

BERTHA BODINE	GLADYS RUSSELL
RUTH MITCHELL	EDITH THORNTON

Music

Chairman, MARION GREENHOOD

ELAINE GRAY	CAROLINE UNDERWOOD
EDNA MOEHRING	MARY WINANS

Program

Chairman, MARGARET MILLER

ELIZABETH BROWN	ELIZABETH JACKSON
GRACE BRIGGS	MARGARET NORRIS

Invitation

Chairman, MARGARET HART

MARTHA BARKER   CARRIE NEWHALL
ALICE HOWE   YEOLI STIMSON

Refreshment

Chairman, MARY STAPLES

MARY BERGEN   SUSIE CALKINS
MAUDE BUSHNELL   HELEN SHERMAN

Ushers

Head Usher, ADIENE BERGEN

OPAL BRACKEN   MURIEL JOHNSTON
KATHLEEN COCKLE   FRANCES JOHNSTONE
EDITH CUTTER   VIRGINIA PEIRCE
ETHEL DUGAN   ALMA SCHLESINGER
JUANITA FIELD   EMILY SMITH
ANNA FINKBINE   PORTIA SWETT
BERNICE HAM   MARJORIE WELLS
CELIA KIMBALL   MAUD WOOLSON

Junior Ushers

Junior Ushers

Mary Alexander
Norma Anderson
Ida Andrus
Ruth Baldwin
Sidney Baldwin
Bernice Barber
Helen Bates
Marcia Beebe
Katherine Bennett
Eleanor Benson
Adiene Bergen
Kathrine Bowman
Elise Bradford
Helen Bradley
Katharine Browning
Frederica Buckley
Hilda Camp
Gertrude Chandler
Breta Childs
Virginia Craven
Marguerite Cray
Margaret Dauchy
Elizabeth Davidson
Alice Day
Helen Denman
Rachel Donnell
Katharine Drew
Abbe Ferrin
Juanita Field
Louise Gates
Mary Geesaman
Marion Greenhood
Gertrude Hawley
Fanny Hazen
Ida Holliday
Annette Hoyt
Gladys Inglehart
Kate Keith
Josephine Keizer
Annis Kendall
Mary Kilborne

Mary Kimball
Helen King
Jessica Lewis
Frances Loney
Mary Luce
Frances Mann
Edith Manning
Louise Marden
Sally McMullin
Elinor Means
Margaret Means
Winifred Metcalf
Helena Miller
Irma Miller
Elise Montgomery
Katharine Morse
Helen Newell
Jean O'Donnel
Caroline Park
Esther Packard
Phoebe Parry
Marion Patton
Jane Perkins
Ruth Perkins
Mildred Perry
Jessie Post
Wilma Ridgway
Edith Riker
Mary Scott
Carolyn Shaw
Winifred Smith
Esther A. Smith
Henrietta Sperry
Laurel Sullivan
Ellen Skinner
Marjorie Talbot
Louisa Van Wagenen
Dorothy Waterman
Katharine Whitin
Elizabeth Wilds
Edith Willetts

Ethel Wilson

10

Big Elm

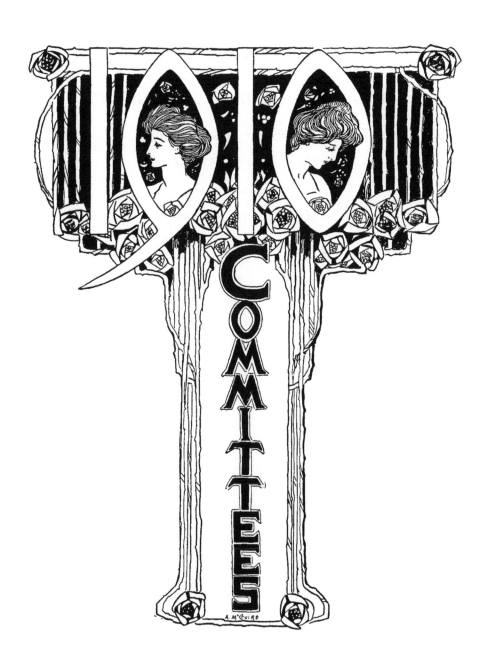

1910

COMMITTEES

A. M^cGUIRE

Preliminary Dramatics Committee

Chairman, MARGARET ELIZABETH MILLER

VIRGINIA CORYELL CRAVEN

FANNY VOSE HAZEN

MARY ALLERTON KILBORNE

GERTRUDE ELIZABETH WILSON

(148)

Senior Dramatic Committee

General Chairman   MARGARET ELIZABETH MILLER
Chairman Committee on Costumes   PEARL EVELYN LE VEQUE
Chairman Committee on Music   MABEL FIELDER HAVENS

Chairman Committee on Scenery { MARY HENRY STEEN*
                              { ANNIS KENDALL

Business Manager   HARRIET FREDERICA BUCKLEY
Stage Manager   FANNY VOSE HAZEN
Advisory Member   HELEN CLEMENTINA BATES
Secretary   WINIFRED CHRISTINA L. METCALF

Costumes

JUANITA EMILY FIELD   EDNA CHIPMAN MOEHRING
ALICE BROWNE McGUIRE   JESSIE WELLS POST

Music

MARION CHARLOTTE GREENHOOD   MABEL LAINHART PARMELEE
RUTH LEONARD   ELSIE IRWIN SWEENEY

Scenery

KATHERINE BENNETT   HILDA MARY CAMP
MARION ELIZABETH BOOTH   HENRIETTA SPERRY

Assistant Business Manager

ALICE FAIRBANKS DAY.

Assistant Stage Manager

ELIZABETH FRANCES NICHOLS

Press Committee

ELOISE RUGGLES CHANDLER   LOUISE KNAPP GATES

*Resigned

A McGuire '10

Senior Pins

Chairman, HILDA MARY CAMP

MARY GRUMMAN WINANS   HARRIET HELOISE HEDGES

Photograph

Chairman, ELIZABETH EDDY

FLORENCE CLARK HAUXHURST   CARRIE WRIGHT NEWHALL

Ivy Song

Chairman, GERTRUDE ELIZABETH WILSON

HELENA FRANKLIN MILLER   CARRIE DELLA WRIGHT

BERTHA BODINE

Campus

Chairman, ETHEL STIMSON

GRACE RUTH MacLANE   LAURA KEZIAH PETTINGELL

Order of Marching

Chairman, VIOLA MARVIN SULLIVAN

HELEN CUSHMAN KING   ARDRA SOULE

MURIEL SEELEY   GRACE CATHARINE BRIGGS

ELIZABETH WOODWORTH JAMESON

Presents

Chairman, ABBE FRANCES FERRIN

MARJORIE ELLIOTT SIMMONS

(150)

Printing
Chairman, VIRGINIA PEIRCE

WILMA RIDGWAY   JOSEPHINE ELIZABETH FRAWLEY
MARGARET ADAMS CUSHMAN   RUTH HOBBY MITCHELL

Commencement Orator
Chairman, VIRGINIA CORYELL CRAVEN

HELEN CHARLOTTE DENMAN   ELINOR HAVEN MEANS

Class Supper
Chairman, DOROTHY WATERMAN

RUTH LEIGHTON   WINIFRED BARBARA SMITH
EDITH MAGDALENE MANNING   MARION ELSIE WILMOT
              KATHARINE CLARK BROWNING

Ivy Day Exercises
Chairman, CELIA ALLEN KIMBALL

GRACE BROWNE McGUIRE   MARGARET APPLETON MEANS
JESSIE LAUREL SULLIVAN   ALICE STEPHANIE O'MEARA
              JULIET ESTELLE VALENTINE

SEELYE HALL

SENIOR WEEK

Cast of "The Winter's Tale"

Senior Dramatics

Cast

Leontes	IDA REBECCA HOLLIDAY
Hermione	LOUISA GODDARD VAN WAGENEN
Polixenes	EDNAH AUGUSTA WHITNEY
Camillo	FRANCESCA BARTLETT
Paulina	PORTIA MANSFIELD SWETT
Antigonus	MARION CECILE WEBSTER
Mamillius	FLORENCE HOYT COLEMAN
Archidamus	JULIET ESTELLE VALENTINE
Florizel	ANNETTE LADD HOYT
Perdita	LOUISE ESTELLE MARDEN
Antolycus	ELIZABETH PLATT WILDS
Clown	MARGARET DAUCHY
Old Shepherd	ELSIE NORA BRILEY
Mopsa	ESTHER ANN SMITH
Dorcas	CAROLINE STINSON BURNE
Neatherd	GLADYS REMSEN VAN DEVENTER
Mariner	JESSIE LAUREL SULLIVAN
Time	ETHEL RAE DUGAN

Baccalaureate Sunday

June 12

Christian Association Services

Music Hall . . . . 9:30 A. M.

Baccalaureate Exercises

Auditorium . . . . 4:00 P. M.

Sermon by L. CLARK SEELYE

Auditorium Vesper Service . . . . . . 7:00 P. M.

Ivy Day

Monday, June 13

Chapel Services	9:00 A. M.
Ivy Procession	10:30 A. M.
Ivy Exercises	11:00 A. M.
Society Reunions	4:00—6:00 P. M.
Art Exhibition	4:00—6:00 P. M.
Promenade Concert	7:00 P. M.
President's Reception	8:00—10:00 P. M.

Ivy Song

PLANT we the ivy vine, heigh O!
    With a sad heart,
    With a glad heart;
Like to our love may its tendrils cleave
To these dear walls we now must leave,
As into the wide, wide world we go,
    With a sad heart,
    With a glad heart.

Fair is the world, and we're young, heigh O!
    Plant the ivy,
    Sing the ivy.
'Tis Springtime of year and Springtime of life,
Skies blue with promise, and hearts that are blithe,
Heeding the voice of the Spring we go;
    Plant the ivy,
    Sing the ivy.

Plant we the ivy vine, heigh O!
    With a sad heart,
    With a glad heart;
Glimpses of shadow and gleams of the sun,
Old joys ended, new joys begun,
And into the wide, wide world we go,
    With a sad heart,
    With a glad heart.

MARGARET NORRIS.

Tuesday, June 14

Commencement Exercises

Auditorium . . . . 10:00 A.M.

Collation

Alumnæ Gymnasium . . . . . . 12:00 M.

Alumnae Meeting

4:00—6:00 P.M.

Class Supper

Gymnasium . . . . 7:00 P.M.

Tuesday, June 14, Gymnasium, 7:00 P. M.

Toast Mistress, ANNE GARDNER PIGEON

'If industriously I played the fool, it was my negligence, not weighing well the end.''
—The Winter's Tale.—Act I, Scene 2.

I. THE COLLEGE AND THE FACULTY ....*Esther Ann Smith*
"I from thee departed, thy penitent reform'd."—Act I, Scene 2.
FRESHMAN CLASS HISTORY ....*Mary Allerton Kilborne*

II. A BOTANICAL RESEARCH—THE ROSE-TREE ....*Grace Browne McGuire*
"I know not how it tastes, though it be dish'd, for me to try how."—Act III, Scene 2.
SOPHOMORE CLASS HISTORY ....*Virginia Coryell Craven*

III. DRAMATICS ....*Elizabeth Platt Wilds*
"Address yourself to entertain them sprightly."—Act IV, Scene 3.
JUNIOR CLASS HISTORY ....*Mary Frank Kimball*

IV. SUFFRAGITIS ....*Marjorie Talbot*
"Be cured of this diseased opinion, and betimes; for 'tis most dangerous."—Act I, Scene 2.
SENIOR CLASS HISTORY ....*Marion Keep Patton*

V. THE CLASS OF 1910 ....*Henrietta Sperry*
"Stay your thanks awhile, and pay them when you part—that's to-morrow."—Act I, Scene 1.

VI. ROLL CALL AND SOME SECRETS REVEALED.
We "shall not need to grieve at knowing of thy choice."—Act IV, Scene 3.

SENIOR - YEAR

If we groan now, O Seniors, at the last, last things of all,
Remember how our summer fun was cut into last fall,
The earliest date possible, as of malice prepense;
But if too early we began, too early we commence.

We thought, being Seniors that we knew the way,—
    One more illusion to join our destroyed 'uns.
        For stop! where are we? where O where is Boyden's?
What! that gay, cosmopolitan café?

For old K. K. then—changed too!—let's seek campus,
    Where these surprises surely can't befall us—
        But will you look at Hatfield fussing Wallace!
'Tis friendly to jog elbows, though they cramp us.

And walls arise where once a hole was all—
    They promise us a Baccalaureate
        Procession down the middle aisle in state,
In this our famous new Assembly Hall.

Enough for us, now, our long hopes' fruition,
    Our library, where we strive to assume,
        While browsing in the Standard Author's Room,
An air of wontedness and hoar tradition.

Let's sing a song of class-meetings,
    We haven't many more.
Our first as "grave old Seniors" we
    Held sitting on the floor.
We chose our Senior president
    And gloried in our choice,
For doesn't Carol represent
    Our *unrescinded* voice?

"Old nineteen-ten" meant something then—
    We found through friendly chatting,
And calm, unbiased statesmanship,
    While working on our tatting,
That all three-hundred seventy-two
    Loved all three-seventy-one.
We went home singing Carols to
    Our great year thus begun.

What shall Dramatics be? is next
   The question that we raise.
Love's Labour's Lost is lost indeed,
   Damned with *one* vote's faint praise,
"Who could play Shylock in this class?"
   No volunteers; we quail.
At last we're sure that we prefer
   "The cut of the Winter's Tail."

More class-meetings.   We chose with care
   Our Ivy Orator
And the committees for the play,
   Then discussed Baccalaur-
Eate attire.   Two factions rose,
   We fought it out between us;
Prexy wants us "in our own hair."
   Ah! has he ever seen us?

Let's sing a song of Class-Meetings
   And hem towels for a trousseau,
For if we don't need them ourselves,
   There are enough that do so;
Or if we'd like to need them,
   We could knit a tie for "brother."
Yes, sing of those old times when we
   Met and discussed each other.

Dramatics trials! bethink you of that time
When weak knees could scarce hold up weaker spirits,
As we crouch'd, waiting, mutt'ring on the stair.
Too soon our names, scarce cognized in our fear
Were called; then had we "tremor cordis" on us,
And we had stumbled in to face the judges.
How the Committee swam before our vision,
Our quondam friends turned ruthlessly to stone;
Tongueless we stood, then stuttered "cues and all"
In tender accents, "What! hast smutch'd thy nose?"
Or in a "monstrous little voice," being five
Feet ten in height, tried for Mamillius,
Or as Paulina, threw the infant down—
In thought to *gently* lay—as 'twere potatoes;
Then 'scaped, we knew not how, and fled in rout.
For some of us,—large sum, alas!—the hazard
Was all for nought—yet had we shown "class spirit,"
And, the cast chosen, we were proud of it
As can the blue-blood Hindu be of his,—
And justly.   Now "The Winter's Tale" is told,

The summer-long its memory shall last;
Again by hearths its lovely spell be cast.

O there's just one class—that's nineteen-ten
    When it comes to Basket-Ball;
You've been three times victor, "ach du liebe" team,
    With the last score best of all,
For there's just one class—that's nineteen-ten
    When you take us all in all.

"The spring, the spring, has come again,
    Once more we stroll the campus dressed in white,"
But now 'tis *we* who hold the steps,
    'Tis *we* who sing throughout the long twilight.
                O happy days!
'Tis *we* who pass between the ivy chains,
    'Tis we who looking in each other's eyes to-night,
Know nineteen-ten means more than all the sum
    Of all we've loved and learned and conquered for the
        right.
                O happy days!

Hopes, eager hearts
    We're bringing now to the unread story
"On, nineteen-ten,
    The even classes are out for glory."

MARION KEEP PATTON

Snap Shots About College

THE PRESIDENT'S HOUSE

COLLEGE HALL

HILLYER ART GALLERY

THE BOAT HOUSE

THE STUDENTS' BUILDING

THE PLANT HOUSE

Music Hall

The Observatory

BOATING ON PARADISE

A FIRE DRILL

CROSSING THE RIVER

ALUMNAE REUNION PARADE

Songs for Rallies and Basketball Games

TUNE: "Fight, Fight for Yale."

On, nineteen ten!
   The even classes are out for glory!
Fight, nineteen ten!
   The ju-ju bird is limp and gory.
The cry is on to victory!
   We'll raise the banner of red triumphant,
Smash! Bang! We'll beat those Sophomores.
   Whoop it up for ten to-day!

TUNE: "Ach du Liebe."

   Nine-teen-ten!
   Ach du liebe, liebe,
   Ach du liebe, liebe,
   We want just one more goal.
   Ach du liebe, liebe,
   Ach du liebe, liebe,
   Just one more goal.

TUNE: "$\Delta K E$ Marching Song."

   Oh! —— —— we sing to you,
   You are so good and true,
   We'll all be loyal to you.
   We'll praise your class
   And praise you too,
   And so we sing
   To 1910 and you.

TUNE: "Jingle Bells."

See them go, see them go,
   Watch them hit the line.
Even classes are the best,
   They get there every time.
   You know it,
      1908, 1910.
Straight and sure their aim,
Pass that ball right down the line,
And we will win the game.

TUNE: "Yankee Doodle."

The ju-ju bird came to the gym,
   His feathers spick and spandy,
He wagged his tail and said "How trim!
   I really am a dandy."

CHORUS.

   Ju-ju, ju-ju, ju-ju dear,
      Perhaps its very naughty
   But oh, we all just love to see
      The humbling of the haughty.

The ju-ju bird was proud and gay
   Till he met the lion there,
And then he lost in some strange way
   His manner debonaire.

The ju-ju bird is pale with woe,
   His spirits vanished quickly,
To Sunnyside he'll have to go
   He is so very sickly.

TUNE: Wesleyan Song "Victory."

Here comes the team girls, cheer them again,
They're going to win for old 1910
E'en if the odds should play a good game
We will beat them just the same,
      Rah! Rah! Rah!
Into the gym they dash to the fight,
Ready to beat the odds out of sight,
While we all cry, "win girls or die,
For you're fighting for the fame of 1910, of
      1910!
Stick to the game, keep the odd classes down.
Fight it to a finish, just do them up brown."
      While we shout victory,
      While we shout victory,
      While we shout victory,
      And 1910 forever.

TUNE: "Hot Time."

1909, do you hear the lion's roar,
1909, we're rolling up the score,
And when the game is won and the Ju-ju is no
more,
Then 1910 we'll be cheering for you.

TUNE: "Upidee-i-di."

1909 is looking sad, tra, la, la! tra, la, la!
I wonder what has made her mad, tra, la, la,
la, la!
Her coaching has been all in vain,
The even team will win again.
Hunta ta, ta, ta! etc.

TUNE: "You're the Girl I Love so Dearly."

"You're the class we love so dearly
Cherish and adore,
You're the class we'll think of always
And honor evermore.
1908 we're singing to you
We're so proud of you,
We're glad to be your sister class
And love you through and through."

TUNE: "He Rambled."

Oh, ten, she has a lion
With long and shaggy hair,
And 'leven has a do-do,
They are a dandy pair.
When these two get together
To have a little scrap,
Just watch the lion swiftly push
The do-do off the map.

CHORUS.

Then they scrambled, they scrambled,
They scrambled on the floor,
They kicked, they bit, they tore,
They scrambled, they scrambled,
The lion gave one loud victorious roar!

TUNE: "Cheer for Old Amherst."

If 'leven must know
Why ten must win
Fight to the finish
Never give in,
Think of the blessing
We have possessing
Our sisters 1908.

TUNE: "Back to the Woods Again."

Back, back, we'll send 'em way back,
Back to the woods again.
Your team may be a wonder
But it can't beat 1910—by thunder.
So long—we hate to beat you,
But we can't help but win,
Any time at all we get that ball,
Well, put it in—yes, yes, way in!

TUNE: "Solomon Levi."

Oh, Dorothy is our captain,
The finest ever seen,
She's here to win for 1910
And beat the Freshman team.
The do-do will be vanquished
And crawl back to his den,
Hurrah for the mighty lion,
Hurrah for 1910!
As we go marching
And the team begins to p-l-a-y,
Can't you hear the people shouting
1910 is out to win to-day!

TUNE: "Back, Back, Back to Baltimore."

Now to Captain Dorothy we will sing,
And to 1910 our praises ring,
By her we'll ever firmly stand.
We're mighty glad to know her, and
To Captain Dorothy we will sing.

TUNE: "Hit the Line for Harvard."

Hit it up for the evens,
Ten must win to-day,
Eleven's team is trembling
The do-do green we'll slay.
Hear the lion roaring,
Hear the Freshmen sigh,
See those bright red banners waving,
As the Sophomore team goes by.

TUNE: "Johnny Smoker."

——— ———, ——— ———,
She can play some,
She can play some,
Watch her play the game of basketball.
Ya, ya, ya, but she plays basketball.
——— ——— ———, she plays basketball.

TUNE: "Princeton Cannon March."

Play, play, with all your might,
And make baskets by the score.
Cheer, cheer for 1910,
As you never cheered before,
Rah, rah, rah, rah!
Evens, sis, boom, bah!
Oh, hear the hoary lion's roar
For we'll play with a vim
That is dead sure to win
For 1910.

What's the matter with ——— ———?
She's all right!
Who's all right?
——— ———.

TUNE: "More Wine, More Wine."

'08, '08, '08, '08, our sister class,
We're glad to have you back,
No other class can take your place with 1910.
We quaff a toast to you we love the most,
And sing with all our hearts to dear old 1908.

TUNE: "Bugle-Call."

'08· —1908, 1908. 1908,
1910, sings to you,
1908.

TUNE: "Glory to Dartmouth."

Glory to '10
Loyally sing
Now altogether
Make the echoes ring for '10·
Our team's a winner,
We've got the stuff:
We have the lion red,
And that's enough!

Song on Taking the Steps from 1909

TUNE: "A Drinking Song."

We take, oh "nine," the steps you leave us,
   As on your way you go to-night;
And though this parting hour may grieve us,
   We'll follow in your steps aright.
With saddened hearts we come to sing you
   A parting song; it is a sign
That we our hearts as tribute bring you,
   We'll ever love you, 1909.

TUNE: "Morning, Cy."

Oh, it's "Odds, good-bye! Odds, good-bye!"
1910 and '12 are feeling spry,
Right on line, just on time.
Jiminy Crickets, but we're feeling fine!
"Odds, good-bye! Odds, good-bye!"
Hear them greet us with the hopeful cry,
"Howdy do!" "Same to you!"
But when the evens take the floor
It's "Odds, good-bye!"

TUNE: "Hail, Hail, the Gang's All Here."

Hail, hail, the team's all here,
Each one up and coming.
They'll start things a-humming.
Hail, hail, the team's all here,
Watch them beat the odds again!

TUNE: "Heinz."

Ten, ten, what's the matter with ten!
'10 is beating it down the floor,
Can't you hear poor '11 roar.
Oh ten, what's the matter with ten!
She's a wonder; hear them thunder;
Ten is winning again.

TUNE: "Score for Yale."

Break up those odd team plays
And score for e-v-e-n.
Straight on across the floor
While 1910 sings Ach, du liebe, ach, du liebe,
Cheer for the team of '10
For they will win.
Push old '11 back, Oh rush them down the floor
And score for '10·

TUNE: "The Girl with the Clocks."

It is four years ago since we first graced rubber
      row,
Timid freshmen, scared and blue;
Rose at dawn to save seats for the Junior's
      day of Prom,
Childish ways we soon outgrew,
As the years rolled along we progressed with
      all our might,
Hidden talents we've developed, in the classics
      we delight,
And some of us are hoping to become efficient
      quite.
In a cottage built for two.

CHORUS.

For nineteen-ten is the class of the latest inno-
      vations,
In a chapel brand new we'll conduct our grad-
      uation.
At baccalaureate simple dresses, no hats, trains
      or frills,
On Rally Day we can't play basketball, they
      won't let us.
But our record of last year won't let them
      soon forget us,
But we're very clever really,
For we leave with President Seelye—
That's in case we can pay our bills!

Oh, 1911 is an altruistic class, to reform us
      they are here,
They'd reform all Smith and the wide world if
      they could.
This to do they have no fear,
Most every week in the note-room hangs a
      sign—
(Spoken) World crisis! how to meet it; Stu-
      dents' Building just at nine,
And, 1911, well we know that sign is thine;
Will you act like this next year?—Cho.

Oh, dear 1912, our little sister class.
You are loyal, you are true.
When we've gone far away and no more you
      see us pass,
Will you miss us as we'll miss you?
In the game to-day keep the even's record clear,
We can't be here to help you but we wish you
      hearty cheer.
And the poor little freshmen will think it's
      mighty queer:
That's the proper thing to do.

There's some cute little girls who have lately
      come to town,
And they're called nineteen-thirteen.
Made themselves right at home, and a-fussing
      big celebs
Very frequently they're seen.
Till exams came along they thought they were
      very wise,
But low grades and conditions brought many a
      grand surprise,
And some of them quite suddenly had trouble
      with their eyes.
But a few are with us still.—Cho.

VERSE

Washington Ode

February 22, 1909

The world lies prostrate, stupefied with woe,
    Her loss not yet all told,—
For Sicily's wreathed uplands no more glow
    With grapes of lucent gold.
From the recesses of the deep there burst
    A force which wrenched, convulsed and overthrew,
      Uprooted Scylla and Charybdis, shook
Whole cities into chaos, dire, accurst;
    To the grim horror added flame, then drew
      The sea-depths up to blot the land out. Look
      Where, without warning sped,
A hundred thousand men, God's creatures all—lie dead.

Yea, and the living, grief- and panic-stricken,
    What worse than death they bear!
Wounded and shelterless, they starve and sicken,
    Reprieved but for despair.
O men have never had such cause to mourn,
    Yet never has the world, one, unified,
      Shared in the grief some of her children knew.
For not by Italy alone is borne
    This loss,—'tis ours, the world's. Our arms stretch wide
      With offerings. Our love is strong to do.
      Though dull to understand
Thy judgments, Lord, in mercy we can trace thy hand.

Across the seas that exiled us of old,
    We hear the cry and come;
With flashing of our word-transmitted gold,
    The great sea-cables hum;
Speeding relief across the severing main,
    The Celtic, richly laden, hasteneth
      To join the fleet form'd not for war, but love,
Where Russians, side by side with men of Spain
    Fight for Calabrian peasants against Death,
      And where our colors. flung with theirs above
      The brightly treacherous sea
Shall form the rainbow promise of a Peace to Be.

To him of Valley Forge glimmered the sign,
    War-dimmed but constant, till
To-day through sorrow it doth clearly shine.
    We must that pledge fulfill,
Who are become all Nations' precedent
    To teach them liberty. O may we not
      Forget that one with it is Brotherhood!

We have been fashioned as an instrument
Of Progress, by the widening of our lot,
To knit mankind together, as God would,
Inheriting the task
Of one whose will was ever the service God might ask.

MARION KEEP PATTON.

The Adventurer

I've traveled a couple of continents, Lass, since the time that you told me no;
There's hardly a port on the face of the earth where it's not been my luck to go;
And I've done things more than a dozen score which no straight man should do;
But whatever I did, I couldn't get rid, dear Lass, of the thought of you.

I've broken nigh all the commandments, Lass, and I've played the deuce with the law;
I have forgotten what "reverence" is; I've lost the meaning of "awe";
And I've broken a handful of hearts or so, while of heads I have broke not a few,
Whatever befell, I met it well, dear Lass—but the thought of you!

I've done strange things, I've heard strange things and curious things have I seen;
I've chummed with an exiled emperor, I've made mad love to a queen;
I've cheated, I've schemed, I've spoiled, I've robbed,—widow and orphan too,—
But what was worse than the widow's curse, dear Lass, was the thought of you.

And things which were never in books I have learned, in odd and devious ways,
And I've put them in use and gained me abuse, honor, and hatred, and praise;
For the devil he loaned me his lore, dear Lass, in return for a soul or two;
But the thing I sought could never be bought,—to be free from the thought of you.

I've led a desperate charge, dear Lass, a madman's raid I have led;
And dagger and knife lent spice to my life, while I lived with a price on my head.
I have drifted for days in a sinking boat with a drunken and frenzied crew,
But I'm not afraid of anything made, dear Lass, but the thought of you.

I have lied in fifteen dialects, I've cursed in a dozen more,
And the sum of the oaths I have broken, Lass, is the sum of the oaths I swore;
I've lost the clean man's way of speech and the clean man's point of view,
But one thing will stay with me for aye, dear Lass, the thought of you!

KATHARINE DUNCAN MORSE.

Lay Communion

The twinkling lights and the crowded street,
The muffled sound of a thousand feet,
The turmoil of traffic, the roar overhead,
My heart feeds full for this is bread.

The golden silence of waning day,
The shaded path in the leafy way,
The world of a thousand dreams is mine—
My soul drinks deep for this is wine.

MARY ELIZABETH LUCE.

My Lady Danceth

My Lady danced; like shimmering light
On the water's breast at night,
As the ripples rise and fall
She danced, and gained my heart in thrall,
For sweet she smiled into my face,
And lured me with her body's grace,
And with her feet she drew me on
Until my heart was wholly won.

O'er the meadows, dewy-wet,
Sweet, my Lady danceth yet!

Swift I did her love entreat,
And laid my heart before her feet,—
She scarcely deigned one scornful glance,
Nor paused a moment in her dance.
Though I warned her, "Raise not hate
In a heart that's desperate!"—
She only laughed in mocking wise,
And scorned me with her lips and eyes.

Where the leaf and sunlight fret,
Gay, my Lady danceth yet!

Then I hied me where there dwelt
A crone who dark enchantments spelt,—
What matter if she took for toll
The one salvation of my soul?
For she wove a subtle spell,
None there was to warn or tell!
Ere three days crept slowly by
My Lady danced—a butterfly.

O'er the meadows, thickly set
With daisy bloom, she danceth yet.

Through the windows of the hall
Where she danced before them all,
(Lord and Lady stand aghast!)
Like a gleam of light she passed.
I, who watched with fevered eye
Gloating, those three days gone by,
Followed as she flutt'ring flew,
Till she melted in the blue.

In revelry that knows no let,
Mad, my Lady danceth yet!

Wind and rainstorm have their will
Of her body, yet she still
Danceth as if for delight,
From the break of dawn till night.
Sun and shower, frost and heat
Pitiless upon her beat;
Still within her magic trance
She floats, forever doomed to dance.

The pains of hell I can forget,
But on my heart she danceth yet.

KATHARINE DUNCAN MORSE.

Questing

They said if we would a hunting go,
    Dorothy Jane and I,
We should find at the tip of the bright
        rainbow
A pot of gold as pure as the snow,
    Dorothy Jane and I.

They said if we listened and listened well,
    Dorothy Jane and I,
Within the heart of a pink sea-shell
We might learn the wisdom the sea-shells
        tell,
    Dorothy Jane and I.

So we looked and listened for we were bold,
    Dorothy Jane and I,
And we searched all day for the pot of gold
And we feared no tale by the sea-shell told,
    Dorothy Jane and I.

'Twas Dorothy Jane found the pot of gold,
    Dorothy Jane not I,
For I who looked till the day grew old
Learned the empty tale that the sea-shell told,
    Not Dorothy Jane but I.

MARY ELIZABETH LUCE.

The Dream-Child

My little dream-child sits close by my knee
    Alone in the dim fire-light,
And we talk of the land of Never-Can-Be
    Till the evening grows into the night.

And ever the fire-light plays on her hair,
    And we talk to each other, low,
Until she grows sleepy, then rocking there
    I croon a dream lullaby slow.

You may keep your children, you mothers true,
    For my motherhood, too, is divine,
And there's all of the roses, and none of the rue,
    With this little dream-child of mine.

MILDRED SIDNEY BALDWIN.

12

Venus to Adonis

Am I not fair?
Lo! all the sunbeams vied
To weave the lustrous fabric of my hair;
And the proud glory of the roses died
When first my two lips curved in mirth.
Am I not fair?
Dost think the bluest flower on earth
Can with the wonder of my eyes compare?

Look long on me, and never shalt thou deign
To cast a glance at mortal maid again.
Draw closer to me; every feature note,
And gaze; until thy heart throbs in thy throat.
Gaze; till the world seems but a phantom place,
Since all its soul is centered in my face.
Close and yet closer! Dost thou now not deem
All thy past life and love an empty dream,
Where all was over in a moment's space?
Lean closer yet; and look into my eyes like sapphires, wet
With nectar, and with this one long, lingering look—all to forget.

KATHARINE DUNCAN MORSE.

Gift O' Dreams

You are asleep, little girl, fast asleep,
  Closed are your eyes of blue,
And over the silence of midnight deep
  I am sending a dream to you.

I am sending you one of a rose, little girl,
  With a pink petaled perfume rare,
That shall hoist a green leaf and a sail unfurl
And sail, and sail on a sea of pearl
  Till it reaches your bedside there.

I am sending you one of an elf,—of a sprite,
  Who will dance in a frolic gay,
Who will win your heart with his glances bright,
And you'll laugh in your dream at the charming sight
  Of the dream-elf's merry way.

And now what dream shall I make my task,
  I who weave as my fancy will?
What would you choose, if you could but ask,
  To have of a dream your fill?

I have sent you one of a rose and an elf,
  I wonder what you would do
If I dared to offer you one of myself.
  Would you want that dream, dear, too.

MILDRED SIDNEY BALDWIN.

Primroses

Pale, chaste and sweet,
  Your dainty leaves unfold,
The strange, wide world to greet
  From tiny hearts of gold.

MARY FRANK KIMBALL.

The Rescue of the Princess

Once when times were quaint and olden, in the days of long ago,
Lived a pretty little princess in a castle built of snow,
And many princes wanted her, their love 'twas very keen,
But it didn't help them any, with a wall of ice between.

And so the little princess lived all lonely and forlorn,
Away inside her castle cold, and wished she'd ne'er been born.
And all the little princes stood outside the castle gate
Warm robed in furs and bearskin, and loudly railed at fate.

Until there came a prince along who saw the princess fair
A standing at her window, and he threw her kisses there.
Then he went and got a polar bear and to his collar tied
A message to the princess, and he sent him to her side.

And the princess read the message, "Lady fair, I love you true,
And I'll rescue you from freezing, that's the first thing that I'll do!
Then I'll marry you, my princess, if you love me, and we'll be
King and queen together, in my kingdom 'cross the sea."

So he went and fought a dragon, and he beat the beastie sore,
And he made him promise truly that he'd roam the world no more,
But he'd follow his young master, and he'd faithfully fulfil
All the prince's plans, and always he would carry out his will.

So the young prince led the dragon rather near the wall of ice,
And the dragon breathed upon it, and 'twas melted in a trice,
Then the prince quick built a scaffold, straight up to the window where
He had seen the little princess sad and lonely, standing there.

And he sent a carrier pigeon, straight into her arms it flew,
And she read, "Climb out your window, princess dear, I pray you do,
Seat yourself upon the platform you have seen me building there,
I'll be with you in a moment. First send down your polar bear!"

Then the young prince led the dragon to the castle's other side,
And the dragon breathed upon it, till the wall seams opened wide,
And the castle all was melted, then the dragon breathed some more,
The water all evaporated leaving there a polished floor.

And the princess on her platform, with her loyal polar bear
Keeping guard down at the bottom, scaring off the princes there.
Then the prince climbed up the ladder, kissed the princess (Lucky Jack),
And they rode off to his kingdom on the faithful dragon's back.

MILDRED SIDNEY BALDWIN.

The Weavers

The robe which Fate was weaving seemed too plain,
Too gray, too dully colored; she would fain
Have had it gayer, brighter with the deep
Crimsons and purples that so often sweep
Across the summer sky when day is done.
So, longing for these joys, when Fate gave none,
She snatched the robe with eager, restless hands
Away from Fate. With many-colored strands
She gladdened it until the garment old
Was swiftly changed to one of shining gold.
All day she wove until the very room
Was filled with radiance, and the busy loom
Was filled with fire. But too dazzling light
Oft blinds the eyes and dims the human sight;
She could not see the flames that round her stole
Until they reached the depths where lies the soul.
Then her heart sickened, and with cries of pain
She called to Fate to come and weave again
The robe of somber gray. Fate shook her head,
But with a smile of pity, cut the thread.

MARY ELIZABETH LUCE.

The Witch Maiden

Pale and fair, pale and fair,
With clinging ashen-colored hair,
And heavy brows that curvingly
Shade my eyes, which more can see
Than a mortal deems is there;
All day long I spinning sit,
Till the glow-worm's lamp is lit,
And the frail stars, one by one,
Shine upon my work, undone.

Silvern bright, silvern bright,
Shines my flickering spindle light:
Flashing in and out it weaves
Magic thread which man deceives
When he deems it pure and white;
For that shimmering thread is wrought
From crafty deed and treacherous thought!
So I smile as still I see
How my web grows speedily.

Singing low, singing low,
As my fingers come and go,
Turns my wheel that singeth clear
What no mortal man could hear
And his heart beat calm and slow;
Witchery and peril dwell
In the song it singeth well:
Ah, beware! lest you should feel
The swift enchantment of my wheel!

KATHARINE DUNCAN MORSE.

The Heart's Abode

Oft has it chanced, as I with careless step
  Passed down among the wonders of the road,
That I have looked through bar and barrier bough,
  And caught far glimpses of the heart's abode.

To one a citadel; to one a shrine;
  To one a wildwood where the sunbeams play,
To some I have won access, and the rest
  I have but marveled at—then turned away.

One day I found you,—in the dusty noon
  The highway lay behind me like a scar,
Before me were cool gardens of delight,
  An unseen hand let down the noiseless bar.

I wandered in, and through long, pleasant ways,
  Beneath the shade of blossom-buried trees,
And saw the butterflies go blowing by—
  The playthings of the perfume-laden breeze.

And gnomes were my companions on the path,
  And woodland fairies clad in gold and red,
And there were elfin shouts, and music wild,
  And laughter in the low boughs overhead.

Upon a rosebush sat a scarlet bird,
  That with a strange song cried unto my heart,
Ah me! its sweetness thrills me even yet,
  Though with the transient sound the ear must pa

And then I knew this was your heart's abode,
  No narrow confines closed in well-wrought stone,
But regions broad and lovely to the sun,
  Where there is peace—and where is peace alone.

And always now beside the dusty road
  I find you,—strangely dear and very fair,
And I,—with every barrier removed,—
  As one the kind gods love, may enter there.

Thou art a garden where I softly go,
  And walk among the fragrant old-time flowers,
And there, where sings the red bird on the bough,
  In you, with you, I dream away the hours.

HENRIETTA SPERRY.

Moonbeams

From still dream fields behind the moon,
Where poppies nod in deep sleep swoon,
And fresh-eyed stars like flowers blow
To the lulled and lapping wind's soft flow:
From the vale of the sheenful moon,
We come, a sisterhood serene,
Bearing dream thoughts all unseen,
Like mystics from some shadow place,
Of strange sweet mien and hallowed grace
The votive nuns of night.
Our fingers thin a blessing shed
Unasked upon the sleeping dead.
We're wandering spirits ages old
Frailly lovely, palely cold,
The ghosts of dead sunbeams.

JESSIE LAUREL SULLIVAN.

Rosemary

A Cupid dancing down Life's path
    Looked in an open door;
He nodded, smiled, and smiled again,
    Then fled, but evermore
There lingered in the tiny room
    The love that Cupid bore.

A thought, quick darting into life
    Elusive, fled my brain,—
I know not rightly what it was,
    Nor why nor whence it came,
I only know the world doth now
    A brighter hope retain.

ELAINE SHEFFIELD WHITMAN.

A "Snap-Course"

In English 13, so they say,
You count in many a funny way—
The time you think, or plan, or write,
No matter if in day or night.
And so, by means of math., I've found
To do no work at all I'm bound,
For though 'tis sixty hours I owe,
Yet all the year it's pained me so
That really I have grown quite thin
Thinking what should be handed in.

And so, by math., as I just said,
I've found that I am 'way ahead,
And not just this year's work is through,
But all I have for years to do.
And now my conscience's free at last,
I'll hand this in to "thirteen" class,
(Not to make up that time, of course,
Nor yet from feeling of remorse),
But just to show my reason's clear
For writing nothing all this year.

MARJORIE TALBOT.

Thoughts in Zoölogy

What do I care for a grasshopper's nerve, or the tongue of a butterfly?
My fingers are busy pinning them out, but I am not here,—not I!
For I lie at full length on the short salt grass on a cliff overhanging the sea,
And over my head a butterfly sways, on wings that are poised, and free.
Far down below comes the swish of the kelp as it floats in the ebb of the tide,
And the shrill harsh cry of a cricket near, hid in the grass by my side.
What do they know of pins and knives, out there with the grass and the sea?
And I would I were out-of-doors with them, and they were not here with me!

MILDRED SIDNEY BALDWIN.

The End of Light

There is a stretch of sunny green unfolding to the hills,
And back of that a row of pines the distant landscape fills,
And back of that the clouds bend low above a purple slope,
And back of that I cannot see—but only dream and hope.

VIRGINIA CORYELL CRAVEN.

PLAYS

O Tempora! O Mores!

Who is this that I now see,
Making frantic love to me?
It's a girl in Section A
I've not seen before to-day!

Oh, to act in Section C,
Where the leading man will be
My own roommate, whom I've known
Ever since I came from home.

But all joys like that are dead,—
I must love this girl instead,
We are both in Section A,
Utter strangers till to-day!

MARY ELIZABETH LUCE.

The Royal Family

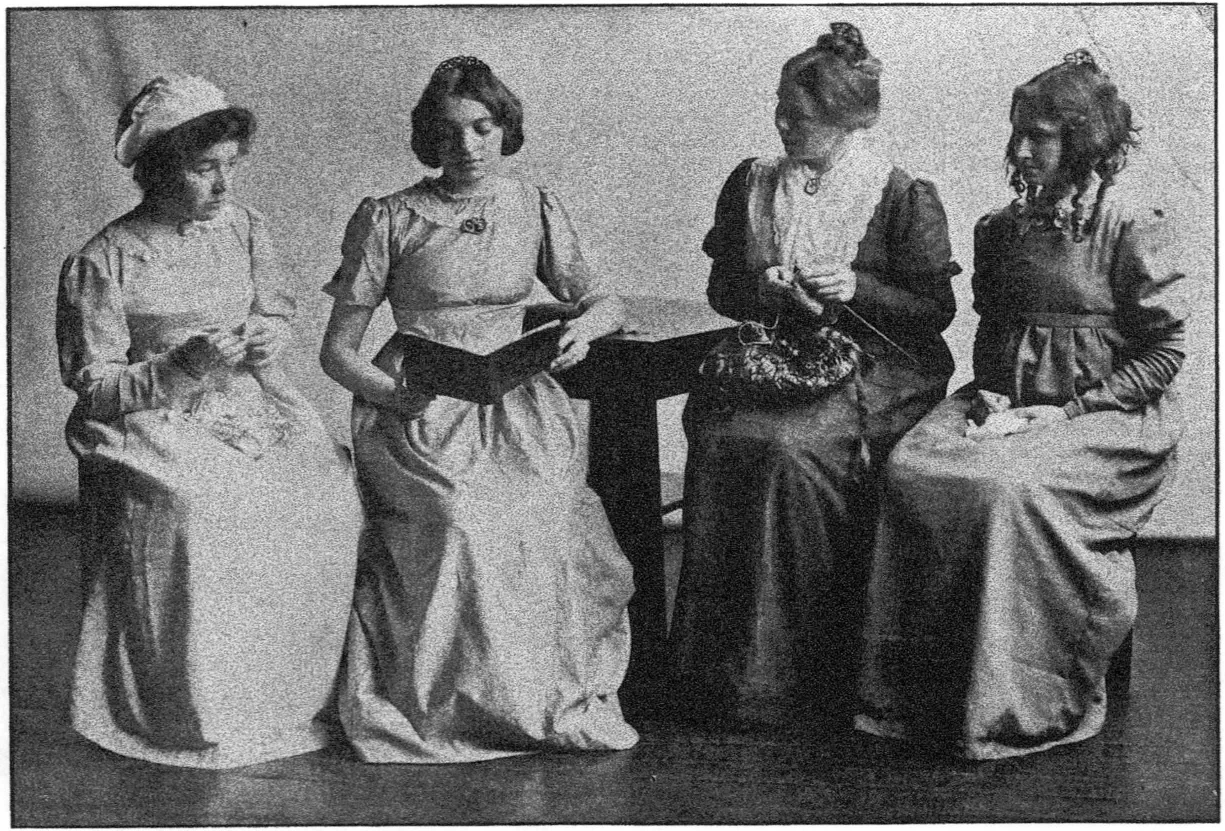

Quality Street

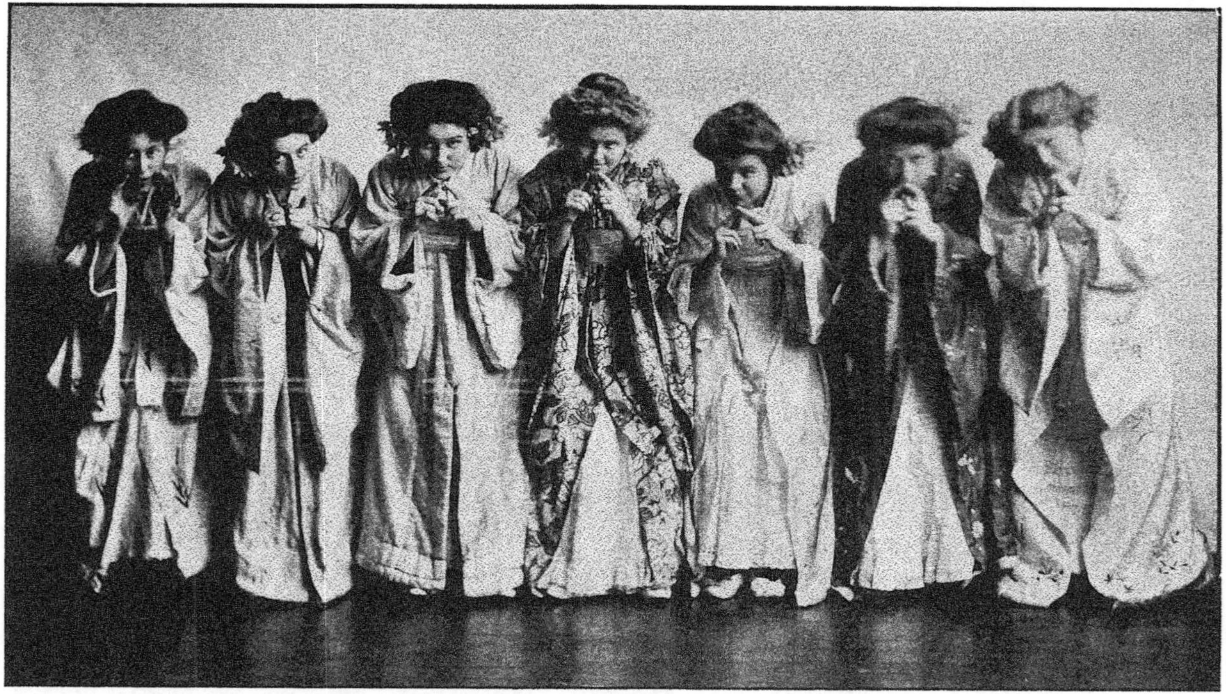

Oh My Land

The Lady of Lyons

CAPTAIN JINKS

OUR MUTUAL FRIEND

Some Things which the College Owes to President Seelye

In "The Dartmouth" for September, 1872, may be found the following item quoted from the "Amherst Student": "Prof. L. Clark Seelye, after a visit to Vassar during their Commencement, has decided to decline the call to the presidency of the Smith Female College at Northampton." "Smith Female College" indeed!—and what happened at Vassar at that fourth commencement?—and what if Prof. L. Clark Seelye had persisted in declining to be president of Smith College?

Nothing happened at Vassar, so President Seelye says, except that he was himself dismayed at the idea of attempting to build or do anything like what he saw there with the amount of money which Miss Smith had left. Compared with Vassar's resources and the endowments of New England colleges for men, her bequest, of between three and four hundred thousand dollars, for building and conducting a college, was plainly inadequate. On that account Professor Seelye declined the presidency.

Without speculating as to what Smith College would have been without President Seelye, suppose we look backward and see what distinctive features in its history and policy may properly be attributed to him. Miss Smith had provided that it should be a real college, that the Bible should be taught in it, that the cottage system of housing the students should prevail, and that men should have a part in its government and instruction. She approved eleven good men and true, who formed a board of trustees distinguished for learning, business sagacity, and liberal views. It is plain that the young Amherst professor of English whom they elected twice over as president, and whose conditions for accepting the office they were willing to meet, must have held in common with them and with the founder, the fundamentals on which the college was based.

From this starting point, President Seelye's first individual contribution to the college was along the line of economy in the expenditure of funds. He emphasized what the trustees fully realized, namely, that the entire bequest was none too large for the nucleus of a permanent productive fund. Although Miss Smith's will provided that half the sum might be used for buildings, he conditioned his acceptance of the presidency on waiting until enough interest had accumulated to build the first necessary buildings. In 1875, five years after Miss Smith's death, College Hall, the President's House, and the Dewey House were ready for occupancy, on land to the purchase of which the town of Northampton had contributed twenty-five thousand dollars. The principal of Miss Smith's gift was untouched, and, I may say here, has never been touched, except to increase it. President Seelye could state at the quarter-centennial, that the trustees "after twenty-five years of profitable educational work, could repay to Sophia Smith, were she living, all that she originally gave, and still retain a cash balance nearly twice the amount of her legacy, besides possessing a valuable campus of nearly forty acres, thirty buildings, extensive library, art, and scientific collections, free from all indebtedness."

The starting of the college without a preparatory department, and with only one class, was a second feature which the college owes to President Seelye. No other college for women was without a preparatory department. Vassar was saddled with one; Wellesley, which opened the same year as Smith, assumed one almost as a matter of course; almost all the co-educational colleges had such departments. Smith College alone began with only so many students as showed themselves capable of doing Freshman class work according to the standard of New England colleges for men. This plan was the result of the study of women's institutions in this country and in Europe, which President Seelye made during the two years before his inauguration. It seems also safe to say that, considering the incredulity with which the public looked upon Greek and higher mathematics for women, it was an experiment that only a young man and one with unusual faith in women would have undertaken. It was consistent with the limited resources of the college. The single class, the members of which pursued the same studies, required only four teachers, few books, and but one recitation room. It was what the college could afford, yet even then it seemed like a great expenditure for a very doubtful issue. President Seelye felt that the college would be prosperous if it could count one hundred students after five years. Certainly his faith in its being worth while was strong that he was willing to spend a fortune on so few.

To the President may be attributed the interpretation which the college has placed upon Miss Smith's direction that the Bible be taught in the college. He at first undertook that department himself, and gave to the early classes lectures on the books of the Bible from a literary point of view, offering a critical analysis of their origin, language, authorship, and relation to other sacred books. Conservative they might seem now by comparison with what has since been learned and written about the Bible, but to one, at least, of the first class to which he gave them, the President's Bible Lectures seemed new and startling beyond anything which she had ever heard before, and marked an era in her life and in the lives of the friends at home to whom she reported them. At the same time, the President's influence in chapel exercises was deeply spiritual, and, long-continued as it has been, has become one of the most important, perhaps the most important, of the sources of his influence. That the college stands for a very inclusive and practical Christianity is President Seelye's work from the beginning. The constitution of the S. C. A. C. W., the interest in missions, and the altruistic spirit of the college, are expressions of it.

The fourth contribution which President Seelye made to Smith College at its start was his attitude toward the general question of women's work and education. Contrary to the almost universal habit of the time, he refrained from expressing any opinion as to woman's sphere or as to what women were capable of doing. He made it plain that he hated the affectations of strong-mindedness, but against the assaults of those who asserted that girls could not study what boys did, that, if they could, it would ruin their health, and that there was no use, anyway, in the higher education except for women who were going to teach, he entrenched himself behind the general proposition that a college education was a good preparation for any career. His eyes twinkled sometimes when we went to him with complaints or requests, but he made us feel like partners in the experiment along with him, and if he thought some of us were strenuous and woefully one-sided, he treated us with a courtesy and our desires with a respect which soothed the sorest and most jealous frame of mind. As a whole '79 took itself very seriously, as, indeed, for the most part, have the alumnæ; but from the beginning President Seelye has known how to deal with ambitious and wholly-in-earnest women, in a spirit in which humor, patience, dignity, and a large view of education have been happily mingled.

No one would disclaim more emphatically than President Seelye that he had made Smith College what it is. To the Faculty is due the Course of Study. Under their intelligent guidance it grew from a single classical course with few electives and the B.A. degree, to the three courses, classical, literary, and scientific, with many electives, and the B.A., B.L., and B.S. degrees, and now again the single degree, B.A., is bestowed for any one of the three courses. The first lady-in-charge had much to do with establishing the character, duties, and importance of that officer. The alumnæ—but I will not enumerate. The college has been a collaboration, trustees, president, teachers, ladies-in-charge, alumnæ, and students working together; but I cannot help thinking that it owes its individuality to its first president, on account of his long term of office, and because from the beginning he has entertained an ideal for women far larger and better than that which any woman would have dared to entertain. Young Smith College is a better expression of all-round womanhood than Old Smith College because of that ideal.

KATE MORRIS CONE, '79

The Secret

I know his power! In his heart there burns
A holy passion like a deathless flame,
For I have seen the kindling of the fire,
The lighting of the tapers in the soul.

I know his gentleness! For in his heart
There blows the white and deathless flower of love,
And now its fragrance sweetens all his ways,
Like perfume from a garden softly blown.

13

HENRIETTA SPERRY.

PARADISE.

mania

(With Apologies.)

The Ellipse! The Parabola! The Frustum!
I exult, I strive, I wrestle with them furiously!
And the charming parallelo "bipeds"
Prance before me.
O the exultation, the thrill of passing planes perpendicularly!
O the thrills of decomposing decahedrons, of truncating prisms!
My intellect bathes in the bliss of it.
Yet my joy is bisected with terror,
I move in hyperbolas of fear
Till the end comes—Q. E. D.

VIRGINIA CORYELL CRAVEN.

I, the undersigned, do on this night, January 18, 1908, being in my right mind and possessed, not of all my faculties, but with fear of all the faculty, humbly make my last will and testament.

Mid-Years To my worthy father I leave all my bills at Bannister's, Field's and Boyden's, and all my money amounting to thirty-three cents. To my mother I bequeath my sewing basket, with all its contents, which are as good as new as I've never used even a needle. To my brother I leave the package of letters tied with pink ribbon, for they may give him helpful suggestions in the near future. (I suppose it would be more romantic if I asked to have Jack's letters buried with me, but no, that isn't the attitude of a college girl. The college woman must sacrifice her own feelings for the development of the world, and I'm sure my brother will find some splendid suggestions in those letters.) I also bequeath to him two volumes of my library, my Carhart's "University Physics" and Greene's "Short History of England." To my sister I leave my jewels, consisting of my precious Bible paper and my physics note-book.

Signed: Pet Ray Fide.

Witnesses: { A Full Moon.
An Innocent Mouse.
A Dripping Candle.

CARRIE NEWHALL.

The Lilly Hall of Sighin's

The Lilly Hall of Sighin's—oh
But learning truth from Nature's slow!
I cannot bear to cut a beetle.
For oftentimes you see its feet'll
Wiggle and wriggle after death,
And it will try to catch its breath.
While as for Physics—(that's required,
For none to choose it could be hired)
You have to measure all the facts
(Ever avoiding parallax).

Now that which I should like to find
'S the *density* of my own mind;
How many *ergs* of work need be—
Work always ergsome is to me—
To help me through that Physics cram;
The *stress* and *strain* of that exam
I never, never could compute,
Nor would I care to, could I do't!

VIRGINIA CORYELL CRAVEN

" Man Wants But Little Here Below "

Little I ask. My wants are small,
One "Merry Widow" that is all;
Cerise and wings—I ask no more—
And just to graze my own front door.

And now that I can swim so fine
Before Gym. faculty in line,
Just one canoe to paddle 'round,
One friend to fish me out ere drowned.

And just one faculty to say,
With two-thirds of his class away,
"Well, bless their simple little hearts,
Spring bats are better than the arts."

But most I want one man for Prom.
I do not care where he is from.
Christian or one-armed Hottentot,
Just one man surely on the spot.

A hat, a boat, a man, a bat,
I ask no more—now say, is that
Requiring too much of the Spring.
When I might ask for anything?

VIRGINIA CORYELL CRAVEN.

The Third Degree

Not satisfied with her A. B.,
  The sweet girl graduate then
Sets out to get a new degree,
  M. A. or M. A. N.

VIRGINIA PEIRCE.

No. 52

Calendar

JANUARY

    6 Opening of the Winter Term
    8 Alpha and Phi Kappa Psi Societies
11-12 Consumers' League Exhibit
  12 Concert by the Olive Mead String Quartet
  15 Open Meeting of Alpha and Phi Kappa Psi Societies. Speaker: Mr.
        Richard Burton of the University of Minnesota
17-25 Mid-Year Examinations
  26 Holiday. Open Meeting of Clef Club
  27 Opening of Second Semester
  29 Clark House Group Dance
      Lawrence House Reception

FEBRUARY

    2 Conference par M. Charles Le Verrier
      Open Meeting of Current Events and Spectator. Speaker: John Spencer
        Bassett
    5 Alpha and Phi Kappa Psi Societies
      Dewey House Reception
      Washburn House Reception
    9 Open Meeting of Biological Society. Lecture by Professor Stockard of
        Cornell Medical College
  13 Day of Prayer for Colleges
  14 Open Meeting of Physics Club. Speaker: Professor W. E. McElfresh
        of Williams College
  16 Concert by Wüllner
  19 French Club Play, "Le Malade Imaginaire"
  22 Washington's Birthday. Holiday
      Alpha and Phi Kappa Psi Societies
  26 Junior Frolic
  28 Discussion. Subject: Pro and Con of Student Government in Colleges

MARCH

    2 Lecture by Mrs. Margaret Deland
    4 Lecture by Miss Mary Van Kleeck, Smith,1904, on the Shirt Waist
        Factory Strike
    5 Dickinson House Reception
    7 Meeting of College Settlement Association. Speaker: Geraldine Gordon,
        Organizing Secretary
    7 Glee Club Concert
  12 Third College Play, "Mice and Men"
  16 Concert by the College Orchestra
  19 Alpha and Phi Kappa Psi Societies
      Gymnastic Exhibition
  23 Beginning of Spring Vacation

APRIL

    7   Spring Term Opens
    9   Morris House Reception
        Hubbard House Reception
  13   Open Meeting of Biological Society
  15   Boston Festival Orchestra Concert
  16   Tyler House Reception
        Baldwin House Group Dance
  23   Alpha and Phi Kappa Psi Societies
  30   Fourth College Play

MAY

    7   Albright House Group Dance
  11   Junior Promenade
  14   Alpha and Phi Kappa Psi Societies
  21   Group Dance
  25   Open Meeting of Clef Club
  28   Alpha and Phi Kappa Psi Societies
  31   Beginning of Final Examinations

JUNE

    9   End of Final Examinations
  12   Baccalaureate Sunday
  13   Ivy Day
  14   Commencement

MILL TOWER IN WINTER

TIFFANY & CO.

Stationery Department

The Stationery Department of Tiffany & Co. is one of the original branches of their business, and since the foundation of the house, in 1837, it has been conducted with special reference to meeting all the requirements of approved custom and usage

The advantages of Tiffany & Co.'s long experience and the equipment of their Stationery Department, are available for the prompt and correct execution of orders for invitations to weddings and all other social occasions and public ceremonies; the announcements of births, betrothals, marriages and deaths; the preparation of dinner cards and menus; the engrossing and illuminating of wedding certificates, testimonials, resolutions and memorials

Stationery for personal, professional and commercial purposes, and for colleges, fraternities, clubs and yachts

Dies of monograms, ciphers, crests, coats of arms, addresses, etc., for stamping on papers and correspondence cards

Guest, log and address books; seals, pads, gold pens, and all furnishings for the desk

Copper-plates used for invitations, announcements, and other social or business forms, converted into photograph frames and card trays, without destroying or obscuring the engraving

Through the facilities of Tiffany & Co.'s Correspondence Department patrons living at a distance are offered prompt and efficient service. A knowledge of what is most in favor at the moment, and of what is suitable for any occasion, assures patrons of intelligent advice and suggestions

The Tiffany Blue Book is issued for the convenience of patrons. It is a compact catalogue, without illustrations, containing over 700 pages of concise descriptions with the range of prices of jewelry, silverware, clocks, bronzes, pottery, glassware, stationery and other goods. The Blue Book will be sent upon request

Fifth Avenue & 37th Street New York

Lightning Source UK Ltd.
Milton Keynes UK
UKHW010428091118
332016UK00007B/177/P